Soundings in Context

The University at Buffalo
Robert Creeley Lectures in Poetry and Poetics
_____

Cristanne Miller, editor

Soundings in Context

Poetry's Embodiments

Edited by

Judith Goldman and
James Maynard

Cover art: Harry Jacobus (1927–2019), untitled drawing (detail), 1993. Copyright © the Poetry Collection of the University Libraries, University at Buffalo, The State University of New York and Christopher Wagstaff. Used with permission.

Published by State University of New York Press, Albany

© 2024 State University of New York

For information, contact State University of New York Press, Albany, NY
www.sunypress.edu

Library of Congress Cataloging-in-Publication Data

Names: Goldman, Judith, 1973– editor. | Maynard, James, 1974– editor.
Title: Soundings in context : poetry's embodiments / edited by Judith
    Goldman and James Maynard.
Description: Albany : State University of New York Press, [2024]. | Series:
    The University at Buffalo Robert Creeley lectures in poetry and
    poetics | Includes bibliographical references and index.
Identifiers: LCCN 2023039273 | ISBN 9781438497556 (hardcover : alk.
    paper) | ISBN 9781438497570 (ebook) } ISBN 9781438497563
    (pbk. : alk. paper)
Subjects: LCSH: Poetics. | Poetry—History and criticism. | LCGFT: Literary
    criticism.
Classification: LCC PN1042 .S68 2024 | DDC 808.1—dc23/eng/20231206
LC record available at https://lccn.loc.gov/2023039273

10 9 8 7 6 5 4 3 2 1

Contents

PART II

Illustrations

Acknowledgments

The editors extend their sincere thanks and appreciation to all who helped organize, sponsor, and participate in the second (2017) and third (2018) University at Buffalo Robert Creeley Lectures in Poetry and Poetics. The Poetics Program is especially grateful to George Life, for his invaluable efforts (including publicity design) around the Creeley lectures as Poetics' graduate assistant, to SUNY Distinguished Professor and Edward H. Butler Chair of English Cristanne Miller, particularly for her organization of the McGann Creeley Lecture, and to James H. McNulty Chair of English, Professor Myung Mi Kim, for her financial and more intangible support of the Lisa Robertson events. Thanks also to the Consulate General of Canada in New York and to University at Buffalo's Office of International Education (particularly then-Interim Vice Provost John Wood) for support of the Robertson Creeley lecture. We are additionally grateful to Cristanne Miller as Series Editor, and to SUNY Press's editorial and production team including Senior Acquisitions Editor Rebecca Colesworthy, Manuscript Editorial Manager Jenn Bennett-Genthner, and Assistant Manuscript Editor Julia Cosacchi. Finally, we would also like to acknowledge the extended period between the events of the third Creeley Lecture and the publication of this volume (in part due to the Covid-19 pandemic), and to thank its contributors for their graciousness and patience.

Introduction

JUDITH GOLDMAN AND JAMES MAYNARD

This volume is the second in the SUNY Press series *The University at Buffalo Robert Creeley Lectures in Poetry and Poetics*. Named for the internationally renowned poet who was a member of the University at Buffalo's (UB's) Department of English from 1966 to 2003 and a founder of the Poetics Program, the Robert Creeley Lecture is now a lecture on poetry and poetics, with accompanying events, featured by the program biannually. These lectures focus on such issues as exploring methodologies or key terms that might reconfigure the operating frames that define current poetic fields; recovering past histories or genealogies of poetics that have been occluded or not yet identified, or constructing futures of poetics; proposing the social, ethical, and political work poetry may do in its potentially spatially and temporally dispersed contexts, vis-à-vis variously situated audiences; and examining poetry's investigative, generative, as well as critical role in language-use and knowledge-formation.

Given this potentially wide range of topics and tenors, and in keeping with the aesthetic values of the UB English Department's Poetics Program, we envision the Creeley Lectures as a discrete series of explorations of different topics in poetics presented by a

1

given set of speakers and respondents in dialogue with a particular audience and through a specific set of programming events—all of which might differ from year to year. The second Creeley Lecture, "Reading Poetry," was presented by the renowned literary and textual scholar Jerome McGann (professor emeritus, University of Virginia, Department of English), whose wide-ranging critical and editorial work traverses the fields of nineteenth- and twentieth-century British and American Literature, Romanticism, Modernism, textual studies, and digital humanities. Focusing on the significance of recitation in Anglophone poetry from the late eighteenth to late twentieth century, the lecture was introduced by Robin Schulze, dean of the college and professor in English, and took place in Baird Hall at the University at Buffalo on March 30, 2017. Also featured at this event were an excerpt from a concert film of SUNY Distinguished Professor David Felder's *Les Quatre Temps Cardinaux*, responding to Creeley's poems "Spring Light" and "Buffalo Evening," and a conversation with the composer, along with a poetry reading by the winners of a high school poetry contest collaboratively sponsored by the UB English Department/Poetics Program and Just Buffalo Literary Center. "A Colloquy on Poetry and Poetics"—a roundtable response to McGann's lecture featuring Alison Fraser, Steve McCaffery, John Rigney, and Nikolaus Wasmoen followed by a community conversation—occurred the next day, hosted by the UB Poetry Collection and organized and moderated by its curator, James Maynard.

The third Creeley Lecture, "*Dous Chantar*: Refrain for a Nightingale," was presented by Canadian poet, essayist, and novelist Lisa Robertson. Author of over twenty-five books, Robertson is known for her innovative, feminist poetics that create highly atmospheric literary spaces, critique gender while performing an erotics of newly imagined relationalities, and produce expansive modes of philosophical inquiry alongside consideration of material culture, often through fascinating engagement with previous texts; she is also a brilliant stylist of lyric prose, whether in her

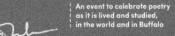
An event to celebrate poetry
as it is lived and studied,
in the world and in Buffalo

Robert Creeley Lecture and Celebration of Poetry

John Stewart Bryan Professor at the University of Virginia

Jerome McGann

Jerome McGann, "Reading Poetry"

March 30, 2017, 4:00-6:30, University at Buffalo, 250 Baird Hall

Jerome McGann is a fellow of the American Academy of Arts and Sciences and of the American Philosophical Society. His twenty-four books and editions have transformed the study of several poets and contemporary editorial theory. His most recent books include *A New Republic of Letters: Memory and Scholarship in the Age of Digital Reproduction* and *The Poet Edgar Allan Poe: Alien Angel* (both with Harvard University Press, 2014). McGann is also a co-founder of the Institute for Advanced Technology in the Humanities (IATH) at the University of Virginia and Director of *The Complete Works of Dante Gabriel Rossetti: A Hypermedia Research Archive* (IATH). His lecture, "Reading Poetry," will track key stylistic innovations developed in England and the U.S. during the Romantic and post-Romantic periods, arguing that these innovations were directed at reimagining the character and practice of human perception.

Also Featuring

Excerpt from a Concert Film of SUNY Distinguished Professor David Felder's *Les Quatre Temps Cardinaux*, responding to Creeley's poems "Spring Light" and "Buffalo Evening" and conversation with the composer.
UB English/Poetics Program and riverrun High School Poetry Contest, reading by winner and runner-ups.

A Colloquy On Poetry and Poetics

March 31, 2017, 3:00-5:00, University at Buffalo, Poetry Collection 420 Capen Hall

On "Reading Poetry": A Roundtable Response to Jerome McGann, inviting scholars, poets, and all readers of poetry to respond to McGann's Creeley Lecture, initiated and moderated by James Maynard, Curator of the UB Poetry Collection. At the close of this event, members of the audience are invited to read a poem—their own, or by a favorite author.

Creeley Celebration
For more information contact
english-department@buffalo.edu

Co-sponsored by UB Poetics Program & Department of English; riverrun; UB Humanities Institute; the James H. McNulty Chair; Comparative Literature; the David Gray Chair Steve McCaffery; Just Buffalo Literary Center; The Poetry Collection of the University Libraries.

University at Buffalo
Department of English
College of Arts and Sciences

Figure I.1. Poster for 2017 University at Buffalo Robert Creeley Lecture in Poetry and Poetics. Image courtesy of the Poetics Program, UB English Department.

Figure I.2. Poster for 2018 University at Buffalo Robert Creeley Lecture in Poetry and Poetics. Image courtesy of the Poetics Program, UB English Department.

prose poetry, fiction, or expository writings. Introduced by Judith Goldman, director of the Poetics Program and associate professor in English, Robertson's lecture took place at Hayes Hall on April 12, 2018. Robertson spoke on the reciprocities between aesthetic form and sociality in Occitan troubadour poetry, contextualizing and theorizing its innovations in rhyme, irreducible multilingualism, intertwined oral-written registers, and its specialized erotic, ethico-political vocabularies, to generate more general reflections on voice, lyric's carrying of repressed histories, and the social affects and epistemology created and mobilized through poetry's soundfields. The next day, a "Roundtable, Community Discussion, and Readings" event, featuring Robertson, with Shannon Maguire and Liz Howard, was hosted by the Poetry Collection and organized and moderated by Goldman, followed by poetry readings by all three.

As a means of expanding the public scope of the lectures and surrounding events, the University at Buffalo Robert Creeley Lectures in Poetry and Poetics series allows us to share these local performances and conversations in an edited format with a wider audience. *Soundings in Context: Poetry's Embodiments* brings together revised versions of the second and third Creeley Lectures by McGann and Robertson, along with responses to those talks by some of the scholars and poets who joined us, and is accordingly divided into two halves to represent each year's lecture and related programming. The volume's first half thus collects extended versions of Wasmoen's and McCaffery's responses to McGann's lecture; the second presents Maguire's and Howard's replies to Robertson's, appearing in their different formats.

For over fifty years, Jerome McGann's work as an editor, textual scholar, and literary critic has examined in myriad and overlapping ways the historical, social, and especially material contexts in which writing is produced and transmitted. In his essay "Reading (I Mean Articulating) Poetry, a Multiplayer Game," based on the talk he delivered under the title "Reading Poetry" as the second Robert Creeley Lecture in Poetry and Poetics, he focuses on a different kind of embodiment: the act of reading a poem out loud. It begins by describing the struggles of students to produce competent readings of poems out loud and their misguided belief that the meaning of the work lies somewhere other than in the words themselves. This fallacy he attributes to the legacy of the influential anthology *Understanding Poetry* (Cleanth Brooks and Robert Penn Warren, first published in 1938) and its New Critical lesson that poems should be deciphered through the various methods of formalist analysis associated with "close reading." The result, he laments, is a body of students who "approac[h] poetry as if it were a vehicle for delivering ideas rather than an expressive, verbal event," and in response he began altering his methods in the classroom to emphasize "the oral ground of the language" through recitation rather than interpretation.

Proceeding from this diagnosis, McGann examines the role of recitation in English language poetry from 1760 to the present, looking at length at how "poetic recitation" was "pivotal" to Wordsworth's *Lyrical Ballads* and its premise that in diction and in prosody there was no "essential difference between the language of prose and metrical composition." McGann shows how Wordsworth's poetics were influenced by the British Elocutionary Movement and in particular his relationship with the poet and educator John Thelwall. For McGann, Thelwall's views offer a basis for understanding recitation as interpretation—and thus a rationale for changing one's methods for teaching poetry to students. A proponent of teaching elocution, Thelwall believed that both poetry and prose were based on an "abstract rhythmus" that shaped the sounds of the language and that by practicing recitation one could become more conscious of and proficient at employing these organizing forces. In Thelwall's view, the reader's spoken articulation of a poem or prose work is an equally creative act of "performative recomposition," with elocutionary "exercises . . . designed to develop an 'instinctive' appreciation and 'perception of the abstract rhythmus' of vernacular English." His aim of teaching elocution was "a recognition of the 'poetic liberty' that the language itself promotes in both writer and reader," with the most effective texts for practicing such enunciative freedom being those with verbal organizational patterns that are both less apparent and mixed, thus placing a greater responsibility on the reader to recognize and interpret them in order to recite them.

Despite what he had written in the Preface to *Lyrical Ballads* about there being no fundamental difference between the language of poetry and prose, Wordsworth would later disagree with Thelwall's valorization of the freedom of mixed measures in recitation and instead argued that, in contrast to prose, poetry depended upon the regularizing effect of iambic pentameter in order to limit the multiple rhythmic possibilities of the English language. However, through a reading of "Michael" and "She Dwelt among the Untrodden Ways," McGann argues that, despite his protestations to the contrary, Wordsworth's writing actually demonstrates the more nuanced and varied meters and sounds that are closer to the compositional freedom of Thelwall's poetics. And in discussing the latter, he observes how certain poems gain their affective significance by presenting the reader with a multitude of interpretive possibilities that no single recitation can ever fully satisfy. In commenting on one's failure adequately to give voice through a single spoken reading to the open-ended possibilities of the lines of the Lucy poem, he writes: "Every effort at recitation, every failed performance, restores the passion of a subject that has no ending."

The rest of the essay largely examines how other poets from the past 250 years have experimented with the prosodic conventions of poetry "to achieve new kinds of rhythms." His examples include the typographical experiments of William Blake's verbal-visual constructions, permutations of the same text in different settings by Walt Whitman, and the exploration of sound in prosaic language in the work of Marianne Moore. In part two of the essay he examines the rhetorical stylings and flourishes of Wordsworth's contemporary Byron, whose epic satire *Don Juan* incorporates multiple dialects of English as well as jargons, words from foreign languages, and established genres, often in the mode of parody. The result is a "polyglot English" drawing upon "multiple cadences" that increasingly exploits the sonic potential of presumably prosaic material like the pharmacological stanza in canto ten. By foregrounding the visual or graphic qualities of language that—like the twentieth-century manifestations of futurist, concrete, and conceptual poetry yet to come—"are better seen and not heard," Byron's work further dramatizes the interpretive decisions and challenges imposed upon the reader in the act of reading aloud. Part three begins with what for McGann is a summary of poetry's innovations since Romanticism: "If any feature of language taken at any level can serve as the measure for its structure, there is no obvious limit to how rhythmic recurrence may be imagined and executed." He then closes with Ron Silliman's theory of the "New Sentence" and its attention to the prosodic possibilities of language at or below the level of the sentence as an organizing structure, which like Byron's work keeps the reader's focus on the materiality of language. And though his examples take him centuries away from the scene of the classroom with which he begins, McGann's essay adamantly demonstrates throughout that the act of interpretation is inseparable from the activity of recitation.

In "'My speech for that unspoken': Recitation and Recognition in T. S. Eliot's 'Marina': Response to Jerome McGann," critic and digital humanities scholar Nikolaus Wasmoen further develops McGann's arguments that acts of recitation are equally acts of interpretation by turning to Roman Jakobson's theory of translation. Approaching recitation as a form of translation from written text to vocalized performance, and citing Jakobson's view of "the interpretation of language more generally" as the translation of one sign into another, Wasmoen observes that both activities "propagate" certain "'metalinguistic' operations" of which a speaker must be aware in order for the processes to be successful. "If we can only speak about what we can speak about speaking," he writes, "then it follows that we can only meaningfully recite a poem to the extent that we can marshal its metalinguistic context." The trouble that McGann describes students having with poetry, then, gets restated here as their mistaken view that these "metalinguistic elements" somehow precede recitation when in fact they are only ever discovered in the act of recitation. Wasmoen then surveys the poem "Marina" to show what kinds of interpretive choices the reader/reciter is forced to make in navigating the multiple source materials (Seneca and Shakespeare) and languages that Eliot weaves together. The reader's participation in recognizing and voicing the particular metalinguistic operations in "Marina," a poem charac-terized by its syntactic subversion, leads to a kind of estrangement that is not unlike the feelings of confusion experienced by the tragic figures of Hercules and Pericles. Wasmoen concludes his response to McGann by considering recitation through the lens of "remediation" as defined by media theorists Jay David Bolter and Richard Grusin, arguing that textual encoding can help pass along "prosodic analysis" to future readers by recording the multiple variations in how a text might be presented and recited.

Presented as a dialogue with specific quotations from "Reading (I Mean Articulating) Poetry, a Multiplayer Game," the contribution by renowned visual and sound poet and critic Steve McCaffery presents a series of micro-responses in rebuttal to the "historical trajectory" of McGann's arguments and obser-vations. In an effort to problematize what he identifies as some of McGann's omissions and generalizations, McCaffery questions whether poetic language is changing in the linguistic world of social media, clarifies the historical development and temporality of concrete poetry, raises "the issue of pronunciation" and the role of "primitivism" for the Romantic poets, considers the relation of John Byrom's shorthand system to Thelwall's practices of elocution, and comments on the apostrophe "oh" that appears in Wordsworth's poem "She Dwelt among the Untrodden Ways." He disagrees with McGann's characterization of Blake's *Laocoön* as an example of concrete poetry, arguing instead that the work is better understood within the context of eighteenth-century political cartoons. McCaffery also adds further proof of the "pentametric pliancy" of Byron by citing lines from Canto V of *Don Juan* and suggests that Italian Futurism as well as Dada contributed to the ongoing history of poetic "freedom." Finally, McCaffery comments on the essay's closing remarks on the New Sentence and argues that an alternative to recitation is the activity of performance as practiced in the work of Jackson Mac Low.

Lisa Robertson's essay "*Dous Chantar*: Refrain for a Nightingale" opens a dazzling view of the world of, and made by, medieval troubadour poetry, framing it through a language politic of "rime." The troubadours wrote in Occitan, an early Romance vernacular with affordances of syllabic stress sensitive to meaning and emphasis not available in Latin, which enabled the poetic innovation of rhyme as technique. Originally both oral *and* scriptural, Occitan developed in a highly literate, polylingual, cross-cultural society, with the troubadours using a specialized, synthetic version of the language in their verse, creating translingual conceptual terms such as *joi* (joy) and *dolchor* (sweetness) that both crystallized an ethics of communality and became nodes for generating intricate fields of like-sounds. Drawing on such scholars as Jacques Roubaud, Paul Zumthor, and Roland Barthes, Robertson writes that troubadour rhyme does not simply name isolated moments of "the surprise of temporal difference in repetition" in a poem, but becomes "an epistemological lens," as she puts it, communicating history. Rhyme refers to how this "active field of the making and reception of verse" encoded an exceptionally culturally and linguistically open, creative milieu's structures of feeling and relation, whose conviviality indeed extended to birds—especially nightingales, so much a part of the soundscape of Languedoc—as co-composers, and blurred the distinction between speech and song.

Robertson is especially attentive to what she terms the *subsong*: the grain of the voice as trace of the body's friction with the material it sounds, which does not appear as meaning so much as it is experienced affectively. She is concerned as well with voice as temporally and psychically riven address, voice as openly relational subjectivity, which partly unknowingly transmits its own historicity as it bends towards its futural interlocutor. This alterity of voice rhymes with rhyme's own potential nonpositive presence, its value produced by resonance or feedback, through "subtextual seeding." Troubadour rhyme thus involves a textilic, nonlinear interlacement that both propels and sends back the reader in a layered, associative gathering of nuance in a process of re-hearing, re-beginning, and re-knowing; this same motion also presences, through reverberation, word-concepts distributed across the soundfield. Such a caressing performance is a parallel enactment of the libidinal social field it illuminates and recipro-cally helps to shape.

Pliny attributed to the nightingale a self-conscious capacity for complex poetic composition, in Robertson's eyes, tantamount to voice, and the nightingale is a constantly reappearing figure in troubadour verse. Yet what if along with Pliny's natural history, she suggests, we might hear in these poems the nightingale as Ovid's metamorphosed, mutilated Philomela? Rhyme performs a cut at which we pivot to re-begin; as Robertson observes, such points of stress also indicate the suppressed space around them—rhyme, as she puts it, "performs a submerged history, in fragments." Because rhyme relies on a formal structure of belatedness, its historical materiality is, too, out of joint with itself, telling the story of its own demise. In its final turn, Robertson's essay elaborates the violent historical rupture that extinguished troubadour culture, when at the beginning of the thirteenth century, the French under papal direction launched a Crusade to end the anti-Church, feminist Christian heretical sect Catharism, as well as the religious and cultural mixing the region was known for. Alongside a renewal of rhyme's communal erotic ethics chez troubadour, she proposes an attentiveness to the cut-edge of rime, the other side of which is loss.

Shannon Maguire's "Making-with Nightingales and Ants: A Response to Lisa Robertson" compellingly traces how the concerns of Robertson's lecture surface in Robertson's poetics, particularly in her recent book of poetry *3 Summers* and her book of essays *Nilling*. Unsurprisingly to Robertson's readers, Maguire turns to Lucretius's *De rerum natura*: a favorite, long-term object of study for Robertson and a source in fact unavailable to the troubadours due to the same Church authority that eradicated the Catharist heresy, but which was nonetheless remotely echoed in their poetry and poetics through its sedimentation in a web of other textual influences. Maguire sees strong affinities between Robertson's creative feminist reading and redirection of Lucretius's atomist materialism and her analysis and reenactment of the troubadour's interspecies poetics of the subsong, noting, for instance that Robertson's poetry "summons new forms and arrangements of letters and sounds, and moves beyond language *as such* to incorporate the sonic fabric of existence and hold space for communications among non-human actors." Maguire helpfully also triangulates the link between Lucretian and troubadour poetics through Donna Haraway's term *sympoiesis*—defined by Haraway as "a word proper to complex, dynamic, responsive, situated, historical systems. It is a word for worlding-with, in company"—particularly interspecies camaraderies. In *3 Summers*, Robertson is preoccupied with hormones and builds a gendered poetics, as Maguire puts it, of "cosmic bodies being phlegmy, oozing, sneezing, dripping entities that spread life in a viral or bacterial way"; Robertson thus plays on and playfully departs, as Maguire reads, from Lucretius's mechanical Epicurean theory of vision as the imprint of films shed by objects, his theory of the clinamen's unpredictable swerve, and his preoccupation with pleasure. Observing "the volatile transformative power of these chemical messengers that affect growth and energy flow among other bodily processes as well as desire between bodies," Maguire in turn draws connections to lines in *3 Summers* that are almost a summation of troubadour poetics: "'What if we've made the wrong use of joy of our bodies? What if / we're to be formal translators of bird cries.'" Akin to Robertson's discussion of troubadour subsong is Robertson's theorization in *Nilling* of noise as a third category, non-value, queerly confounding the distinction between sound and silence.

The transcript of the lively roundtable discussion of *"Dous Chantar"* featuring Robertson, Maguire, and Howard focuses largely on language politics and language endangerment. Profoundly influenced by her poetics and more personally by Robertson as mentor, Maguire and Howard were invited to respond to the lecture by linking it to their own thought and practice. At the roundtable, Maguire delivered an early version of the essay included here, followed by remarks by Howard, and then by conversation amongst the panelists and the audience. In her discussion, Howard recurs to Robertson's image of Philomela's severed tongue, in turn setting forth the striking notion of revenants of the dead in the land as providing physical and metaphysical nutriment, from which she explores the *topos* of the transformational returns of cultures traumatized even to the point of extinction. One way her first book *Infinite Citizen of the Shaking Tent* is bound up with her First Nations heritage is through its relation of "survivance" (Gerald Vizenor) or "resurgence" (Leanne Simpson) to the near-lost, sacred, oracular Ojibwe practice of *jiisakaan*, "shaking tent," in which a human "conjuror" gathers information from an animal spirit who acts as translator of other animal spirits speaking in their separate vernaculars. As Howard describes, her own practice of making her work involves processes of taking in and then translating information received (implicitly through felt presences). Relatedly, through Jacques Roubaud's *The Loop*, Howard theorizes refrain as a destructive-constructive mode of remembrance, in which retrieval does not simply repeat but corrodes and transforms, registering the act of memory itself.

As the conversation turns to reflect on how the distant past speaks through us in our positions, for instance, as descendants of White settlers and Indigenous peoples, Robertson notes parallels between medieval crusades and settler colonialism, as well as with Fortress Europe's treatment of refugees, so many of whom are cruelly left by states to perish en route. Refrain returns to the discussion, reframed as the deterritorializing "line of flight" in poetry that refuses monolingualism and other purifications of territory. What do language regimes we've internalized regulate or disallow? Should proficiency be what permits us to speak a language, or might we embrace amateur speakership (across multiple meanings of *amateur*)? How do we move in between languages as conditioned by context and interlocutor(s), and what are the politics of "improvising across latins"? Continuing Robertson's investigation of the subsong, and the historicity of the affective materiality of language, the poets discuss rhyme as bearing the "nonvolitional texture" of the past. Wordplay in troubadour poetry also comes to the fore as Robertson alerts us to archives of drafts in which poems are inscribed on the page in "precodified" ways, generating webs of association and meanings. While rhyme shifts the temporality of our experience of a text, the synesthesia of wordplay brings the body to the fore in the act of reading.

∾

While the lectures simply followed each other in the series, they nonetheless make good companions, with significant echoes reverberating between them and their accompanying responses.

The lecturers and their immediate interlocutors all are concerned with voicing in context; various kinds of lability of the poetic text and what produces the possibility of its differential expressivity; sonic patterning in poetry and its modes of significance; and the foregrounding of an embodied experience of oral and written language, versus its interpretation. All of these contributions propose affective, pragmatic approaches to poetry that allow it to surface as materially formative, alive and lived. Reading them together offers an opportunity to see how these values presence themselves in differing cultures of poetic scenography across space and time.

PART I

Chapter 1

2017 Robert Creeley Lecture in Poetry and Poetics

Reading (I Mean Articulating) Poetry, a Multiplayer Game

JEROME MCGANN

I.

My subject today is poetry and how my students do and don't deal with it. Two refrains are common: "I hate it" and "It's too hard, I don't understand it." And they will prove the truth of those judgments (alas!) when they read passages during classroom discussions. It's a virtually universal and painful experience for everyone. Few can manage a competent recitation and virtually none understands why recitation is important. Very often they have the greatest difficulty even articulating the words of a language they otherwise—beyond poetry—know pretty well.

It took me years to discover one important aspect of this problem. The students hardly think of poetry as part of their language at all. It seems to them a kind of code that has to be deciphered. Because they often take it for granted it is saying—or at least meaning to say—profound things (that's in itself another

19

part of the problem), they're put off by poetry: either peeved or intimidated. So classes turn beleaguered for everyone. Because the students are perfectly certain that *I* understand these strange works, they approach them with their eyes on me—as if their eyes were watching a god who would approve (or not) their brave and pitiful efforts to penetrate the mysteries.

About fifteen years ago I began to change what we were doing in my undergraduate classes. If I were entirely honest about the problems here I would have made similar changes in my graduate classes, where competence in reading poetry is only a bit better. But it's hard to tell young people who have just launched themselves into such a vocation as ours that they have some elementary *un*learning to do about "literature," poetry as well as prose. So I tread more softly there. But with the undergraduates I decided to bite the bullet. My poetry classes wouldn't be about *interpreting* poetry any more but about *reading* poetry. Recitation. Memorization. Oral articulation of the language.

I realize now, much after the fact, that I crossed this Rubicon because of what the best students in my classes were doing. They were no better or worse at *reading* the poetry aloud but they definitely knew something about how to decode. Those best students—if "best" is the right word here—would scrutinize a poem's formal and content features in an effort to give an account of its thematic organization.

These students had learned the basic lesson passed down by the single most influential modern book of poetry education—Cleanth Brooks and Robert Penn Warren's *Understanding Poetry*, which went through four editions (1938–1976) in scores of thousands of copies. It has been well said by a contemporary scholar and educator that "a poem is the language of an act of attention."[1] *Understanding Poetry* and its many offspring—by no means only "New Critical" offspring—urged readers to give close intellectual attention to how the poem worked. It was a reasonable premise of the entire program that word-works crafted with the deliberation of poems would set a model for improving our understanding of language itself, our basic means of communicative exchange and social intercourse. A not irrelevant bonus would be the cultural uplift—"Cultural Literacy"—that came from a regular commerce with "the best that has been known and thought in the world" (Matthew Arnold).

And yet the inability of those same students to articulate the poetry made it plain that in certain fundamental respects, all types of "close reading" were failures. Even "the best" students kept approaching poetry as if it were a vehicle for delivering ideas rather than an expressive, verbal event. Mallarmé's famous reply to Degas's complaint that he couldn't get his sonnet to deliver his ideas remains deeply pertinent: "But Degas, you can't make a poem with ideas. . . . *You make it with words*."[2] Poets, especially over the past two hundred years, have learned complex ways to turn the bibliographical presentation of words into an expressive event. But even as that takes place—in concrete poetry, for example, as we shall see—the oral ground of the language remains fundamental.

Many complex social forces and circumstances contribute to the situation I'm describing. While those matters matter to me as much as to anyone, they aren't my focus here. Rather, I want to report on the effect this turn to recitation had on my own understanding of poetry, and in particular on poetic practices from about 1760 to the present. (I start at 1760 because that's the year James Macpherson published the first of his enormously influential volumes of Ossianic prose poetry, *Relics of Ancient Poetry*.)

It is a truth universally acknowledged, at least among scholars, that the period from 1760 is marked by two major and related upheavals, one called Romanticism, the other, Modernism. So far as English poetry is concerned, Wordsworth—and in particular the *Lyrical Ballads* project—turned out to be a recognizably decisive event. As the poetry of that famous book showed, and its equally famous "Preface" told, Wordsworth argued for a fundamental reconsideration of poetic expression. The issue involved Wordsworth's view of the appropriate "language" for poetry. He argued that two specific matters—poetic diction and poetic prosody—were pivotal and that both flourished under the idea "that there neither is, nor can be, any essential difference between the language of prose and metrical composition." Here is the relevant passage: "Prose [is the] natural or regular part of [a] language [so that] the language of every good poem can in no respect differ from that of good prose. We will go further. It may be safely affirmed, that there neither is, nor can be, any essential difference between the language of prose and metrical composition."[3] Perhaps no comment by an English poet has been more consequential than that. Reading it now we can hardly not think of the downstream watershed of free verse, prose poetry, and even concrete poetry.

But what brought Wordsworth to make his famous declaration? It turns out that the issue of poetic recitation was pivotal. When Wordsworth writes about "the language of every good poem," the language he has in mind is spoken, not literary, English. More, it is the spoken prose "really used by men [in] low and rustic life" (Gill, 597). Coleridge was as deeply involved in the *Lyrical Ballads* project as Wordsworth, but he sharply demurred from his friend's "rustic life" model for good prose, parodying Wordsworth's phrasing brilliantly: "there may, there is, and ought to be, an essential difference between the language of prose and metrical composition."[4] Soon after he published his "Preface" Wordsworth himself beat a notable retreat from what he had written, as we shall see. But he seized that model because his ambition was toward what he called "philosophic song" (*The Prelude*, Book I, 230; Gill, 380). He was arguing that simpler forms of vernacular English were "more truly philosophical" than what he called the "barren leaves" of the natural and moral philosophical works so prominent at the time.[5] Though Thomas Love Peacock had yet to issue his 1820 manifesto declaring that "a poet in our times is a semi-barbarian in a civilized community"

(*The Four Ages of Poetry*), Wordsworth and Coleridge from 1797 forward were writing under threat of just that kind of confident, late Enlightenment progressivism.[6]

Wordsworth's "Preface" was arguing that poetry's place in the modern "civilized community" was tied to its exemplary care for the language. His general frame of reference was the immensely consequential British Elocutionary Movement, where language study and education were grounded in systematic approaches to recitation. More particularly, during the crucial years 1797–1804 both Coleridge's and Wordsworth's thinking about poetry and language was being pressured and shaped by their conversations with John Thelwall, the radical poet and educator whose work came directly out of the Elocutionary Movement.

The movement worked from two related ideas, one theoretical, one practical: first, that all forms of linguistic expression, oral or otherwise, prose and verse, draw upon and play with an "abstract rhythmus" that organizes the language;[7] and second, that this abstract rhythmus will remain an unheard melody, an unavailable reader's resource, without repeated recitational practice. Wordsworth's interest in spoken language rests in his view, which he shared with Coleridge and Thelwall, that current literary work had sophisticated itself out of all awareness of the truth of oral expression and the human intercourse it made possible.[8]

A poet himself, Thelwall shared Wordsworth's and Coleridge's concerns about poetry and elevated forms of cultural practice. But he set those interests in a far more extensive social context. He became a community educator promoting language competence for everyone. People from all classes and walks of life attended his lectures and took his instructional courses. (Indeed, because of his working-class background he was often attacked and vilified for such presumption.) I don't mention this difference to praise Thelwall at the expense of his friends' political conservatism. He greatly admired, though not uncritically, both men and was for a time intimate with both. But considered strictly from the point of view of the history of English poetry since 1760, Thelwall's community work is deeply pertinent. It signals his view that two parties had to be involved in what Wordsworth's "Preface" called the "engagement" contracted between poet and reader (Gill, 596). Readers were to be agents of change as well poets, and "reading poetry"—giving it an articulated form—was essential. Indeed, it was another mode of poetic "composition."

While Thelwall uses literary texts in his exercises, the focus is promoting "perfect liberty" of expression in reading, speaking, and writing. "Flexure and harmonic variety are the perpetual objects of the system" (*Illustrations*, xxvi). His "elocutionary instruction" is grounded in texts drawn from as wide a variety of English authors, prose and verse, as possible—the goal being a recognition of the "poetic liberty" that the language itself promotes in both writer and reader (*Illustrations*, xix). For Thelwall, while this "poetic liberty" is most perfectly realized in Milton and Shakespeare, they "are not . . . the authors with whom [to] begin [the study of English verse and prose]. They are the pillars of the temple, rather than the foundation" (*Illustrations*, xviii).

Thelwall's exercises were designed to develop an "instinctive" appreciation and "perception of the abstract rhythmus" of vernacular English (*Illustrations*, xxiii)—a *feeling* for the language quite akin to what William Carlos Williams would later call "embodied knowledge."[9] Like Wordsworth in the "Preface," Thelwall was working from associationist ideas about the importance of developing reliable "habits" of attention and responsiveness (Gill, 598). He developed a graduated regimen in the notation and recitation of a wide variety of "illustrations" of English prose and verse. Prose turned out to be especially important exactly because its "abstract rhythmus" (videlicet, its metrical order) was so much less apparent than versified language: "As prose is made up of unequal fragments of all kinds of measures, he who would utter it well, should be familiar with all kinds of varieties, and should seek them there where their qualities are most ascertainable, and their peculiarities are most easily comprehended. He should do more—to complete his perception of rhythmus, and improve the flowing variety of his style, he should learn to compose in all" (*Illustrations*, xx). The first sentence tells us why articulated prose became such a focus of attention for Thelwall and Wordsworth: it "is made up of unequal fragments of all kinds of measures." The comment implicitly forecasts the experiments in free verse, prose poetry, and concrete poetry that will be feeding off that remarkable insight throughout the next two hundred years. But the second sentence is talking about something that preoccupied only Thelwall. The key word is "compose." For Thelwall, recitation exercises are a form of performative recomposition, a completion of the "engagement . . . contracted" between poet and reader.

What is involved here gets further exposed in Wordsworth and Thelwall's 1804 letter exchange about poetry. Although Thelwall's letter is no longer extant, Wordsworth's reply leaves no doubt about a key issue being discussed. Wordsworth wrote to warn Thelwall about "the error you [Thelwall] have fallen into, [ov]er verse mouth and prose mouth."[10] Working from certain regulative ideas promoted in the Elocution Movement, Thelwall was discussing the importance of not distinguishing between "a verse mouth and a prose mouth": "I want only a distinct, a sonorous, an articulative mouth—a mouth that 'is parcel of the mind,' and of a mind that can identify itself with its author, or its subject" (*Illustrations*, xvi).

Wordsworth replies that "I never used [such] phrases in my life, and hold no such opinions." Despite what he had written about prose and verse in his 1800 "Preface," he was now resisting the implications of Thelwall's very similar ideas.[11] Recognizing that "your general rule is just that the art of verse should not . . . violat[e] the nature of Prose," he warns that "this rule should be taken with limitations." Against Thelwall he briefly sets out his own "system of metre," which he calls "very simple," following, as he tells Thelwall, "the regular laws of the Iambic."

If Thelwall's ideas were to prevail, Wordsworth argues, he could conceive "scarcely . . . any limits to the dislocation of the verse by some passion or other." The regular laws of iambic versification are necessary to prevent "the passion of the subject" from destroying the order of the verse, or what he calls "the passion of [the] metre." But Thelwall's point is that refusing the distinction between prose and verse provides the basis for a more nuanced register of the "laws" of tempo, pitch, and stress established at the language's basic lexical, grammatic, and phonemic levels. One might invoke here a relevant term from traditional versification—logaoedic—and argue that Thelwall (and in my judgment, Wordsworth as well, at least in his poetry) was registering his language's special predisposition to logaoedic rhythms: that is, verse in which mixed meters are combined within a single line to give the effect of prose.[12] Both men had a deep intuition for the "abstract rhythmus" of vernacular English, or what Keats would later call "the true voice of feeling."[13]

Wordsworth wanted rhyme, lineation, and iambic law ("the passion of metre") to collect and recollect "in tranquility" his subject's—his own—"powerful feelings" (what he calls "the passion of the subject" in his letter to Thelwall).[14] Indeed, it is not just meter—and, more specifically, iambic law—that Wordsworth begs for, but a conventional typography that will openly declare the authority of his literary heritage. Like all the British elocutionists, Thelwall rejected the methods of traditional scansion in favor of an analytic method drawn from musical notation. Traditional scansion not only failed to supply a nuanced account of English cadences and rhythms, it was obscuring the truth of poetic expression and representation at every level, even "deform[ing] our typography [and] corrupt[ing] our orthography."[15]

In his letter to Thelwall, Wordsworth is quite aware that a traditional approach to prosody and "the law of the Iambic" is related to the printed disposition of the text: "as long as verse shall have the marked termination that rhyme gives it, and as long as blank verse shall be printed in lines, it will be physically impossible to pronounce the last words or syllables of the lines with the same indifference as the others."[16] But Thelwall's view is that if poets compose poetry and readers recompose it as Wordsworth is suggesting, they will lose access to the "abstract rhythmus"—the unheard melodies—of a language rife with many rhythmical possibilities, many possible pronunciations. As Blake would write, "Bring out Number Weight & Measure in a year of Dearth" (*The Marriage of Heaven and Hell*, plate 7). Indeed, when end rhyme and syllabic lineation no longer lay down the law to poetic composition and reception, the doors of reception get thrown open to the "perfect freedom" Thelwall found in Milton and Shakespeare.

The truth is that Wordsworth's own practice in those crucial years was already producing what he thought—and perhaps sometimes feared?—was impossible. The opening passages of "Michael" and "Tintern Abbey" show Wordsworth uplifting the words and syllables of his verse to different prosodic—and meaningful—values:

> If from the public way you turn your steps
> Up the tumultuous brook of Greenhead Ghyll,
> You will suppose that with an upright path
> Your feet must struggle; in such bold ascent
> The pastoral mountains front you, face to face.
> But, courage! for around that boisterous brook
> The mountains have all opened out themselves,
> And made a hidden valley of their own. ("Michael,"
>   lines 1–8; Gill, 224)

Not only does iambic law *not* govern the cadential movement of those lines, they issue a positive invitation to leave that "public way" behind. The passage is a call for—a kind of allegory about—a poetry "made up of unequal fragments of all kinds of measures."

The lines have "opened out themselves" to various possibilities for tempo, stress, and pitch. "Tumultuous" may throw out the syllable count and the iambic rhythm, "But, courage," for something unusual is happening here. Raiding the iambic and pentametric treasures, Wordsworth is already breaking the law.

Here is an exercise: write out those lines margin-to-margin. So organized, they will recall what Dr. Johnson, quoting William Lock, thought to say of Milton's blank verse: that it was "verse only to the eye" ("The Life of Milton").[17] And because the diction is not elevated, like Milton's, the prosaic effect is yet more striking. If one then proposes to execute a recitation, the cadence alternatives leap to attention and lay down serious interpretive demands.

The works from this period that are perhaps most remarkable may not be Wordsworth's blank verse poems like "Michael" and *The Prelude*, but those brief and magical texts crafted by the "Simple Wordsworth":[18]

> She *lived* unknown, and few could know
> When Lucy ceas'd to be;
> But she is in her Grave, and oh!
> The difference to me. ("She Dwelt among
> Untrodden Ways," Gill, 148)

Certainly the passage works a "tension" between the passion of the meter and the passion of the subject. That is set up in the first two lines, though the first line fairly announces that "unequal measures" are in play. But the law of the iamb gets overridden in the final two lines, where none of the words suffer what Wordsworth called "indifference," as the fully articulated word "difference" makes especially clear. Crucially, that final line—whose cadence outrides through two stresses—is feeding off the five insignificant words that launch the momentous rhythm of the third line. While that line delivers, incidentally as it were, the suggestive off-rhyme *lived*/Grave, its force comes through the different affective (affecting) ways each of those little words might be *read*. The uncanny success of the passage is a function of the impossible demand that line makes for a completely satisfactory recitation. It is not the law of the iamb that licenses such articulate energy, it is the historical fate of the language itself—"the common risks of language, where failure stalks in every word."[19] Failure stalks because options loom through words—even the smallest words—"made up . . . of all kinds of measures." As I read those verses now, I am once again struck dumb by their perfect expression of loss. Every effort at recitation, every failed performance, restores the passion of a subject that has no ending.

"As long as verse shall have the marked termination that rhyme gives it, and as long as blank verse shall be printed in lines," Wordsworth told Thelwall, the distinction between verse and prose will remain intact and the iambic law will rule. But the time was soon to come when poets would simply drop those typographical expectations or play with them to achieve new kinds of rhythms. Unbeknownst to Wordsworth and nearly all of his contemporaries, Blake was already doing it. Everything about *The Marriage of Heaven and Hell* (1790–1793) represents an attack on those conventions.

A free verse poem emerges on the plate because Blake is exploiting the plate's four spatial coordinates (see figure 1.1). All of his subsequent illuminated works fracture and mutate various kinds of traditional verse models in similar ways. Ossian, ancient hexameter verse, and early English heptameters turn into the lyrical prose poetry of his two culminant masterpieces—the famous "wall of words" that rise up in *Milton* and *Jerusalem* (see figure 1.2).[20]

And then there is the astonishing *Laocoön* (c. 1826–1827), which is manifestly an instance of what we now call concrete poetry (see figure 1.3).

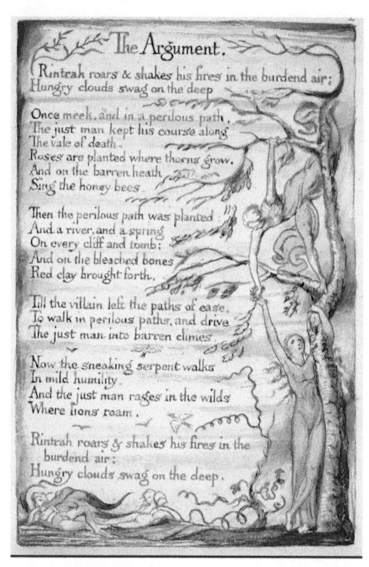

Figure 1.1. William Blake, *The Marriage of Heaven and Hell*, plate 2 (Copy G). Reprinted courtesy of the William Blake Archive, http://www.blakearchive.org.

Figure 1.2. William Blake, *Jerusalem*, plate 10 (Copy E). Reprinted courtesy of the William Blake Archive, http://www.blakearchive.org.

Figure 1.3. William Blake, *Laocoön*, Copy B. Collection of Robert N. Essick. Copyright © 2023 William Blake Archive. Used with permission.

Two sets of downstream examples—one out of Whitman, the other from Marianne Moore—need little comment since their face values carry the point. The Whitman passages are three prose-poetical versions of the same basic text. The first comes from the untitled prose poem known as the "Preface" to the 1855 *Leaves of Grass*; the second from the "Poem of Many in One" (in the 1856 edition of *Leaves of Grass*); and the third from "By Blue Ontario's Shores" (in the 1860 edition of *Leaves of Grass*).[21]

> This is what you shall do: Love the earth and sun and the animals, despise riches, give alms to every one that asks, stand up for the stupid and crazy, devote your income and labor to others, hate tyrants, argue not concerning God, have patience and indulgence toward the people, take off your hat to nothing known or unknown or to any man or number of men, go freely with powerful uneducated persons and with the young and with the mothers of families, read these leaves in the open air every season of every year of your life, re examine all you have been told at school or church or in any book, dismiss whatever insults your own soul, and your very flesh shall be a great poem and have the richest fluency not only in its words but in the silent lines of its lips and face and between the lashes of your eyes and in every motion and joint of your body. ("Preface," 1855 *Leaves of Grass*)

> I have loved the earth, sun, animals—I have de-
>   spised riches,
> I have given alms to every one that asked, stood
>   up for the stupid and crazy, devoted my in-
>   come and labor to others,
> I have hated tyrants, argued not concerning God,
>   had patience and indulgence toward the peo-
>   ple, taken off my hat to nothing known or
>   unknown,
> I have gone freely with powerful uneducated per-
>   sons, and with the young, and with the
>   mothers of families,

I have read these leaves to myself in the open air,
I have tried them by trees, stars, rivers,
I have dismissed whatever insulted my own soul
        or defiled my body,
("Poem of Many in One")

I have loved the earth, sun, animals, I have despised
        riches,
I have given alms to every one that ask'd, stood up
        for the stupid
                and crazy, devoted my income and labor to others,
Hated tyrants, argued not concerning God, had
        patience and
                indulgence toward the people, taken off my hat to
                nothing known or unknown,
Gone freely with powerful uneducated persons and
        with the young,
                and with the mothers of families,
Read these leaves to myself in the open air, tried
        them by trees,
                stars, rivers,
Dismiss'd whatever insulted my own soul or defiled
        my body,
("By Blue Ontario's Shores")

The most famous Moore example would be what she did with her 1924 signature work "Poetry"—a poem successively stripped bare of its free verse, even, and reduced in 1967 to a stringent prose-poetical dictum:

I, too, dislike it.
        Reading it, however, with a perfect contempt for
        it, one discovers in it, after all, a place for the
        genuine.[22]

Or consider how she altered "The Fish" from its 1918 to its 1919 version. The opening passage will suffice for illustration:

The Fish

Wade through black jade.
Of the crow-blue mussel shells, one
Keeps adjusting the ash-heaps
Opening and shutting itself like
(*The Egoist* text, 1918)[23]

The Fish

wade
through black jade.
    Of the crow-blue mussel-shells, one
      keeps
      adjusting the ash-heaps;
    opening and shutting itself like
(*Others for 1919* text)

Those stanza patterns recur through the rest of those versions of the poem. The texts are definitely verse only for the eye and the eye of the mind, as we see very clearly when we write them out as margin-to-margin prose. I give a more extended piece of the poem's opening to make the prosaic order of the poem unmistakable: "The fish wade through black jade. Of the crow-blue mussel shells, one keeps adjusting the ash-heaps, opening and shutting itself like an injured fan. The barnacles which encrust the side of the wave cannot hide there, for the submerged shafts of the sun, split like spun-glass, move themselves with spotlight swiftness into the crevices, in and out, illuminating the turquoise sea of bodies."[24] Setting that typographical deployment alongside Moore's typographies makes her point. She is exposing the metrical resources—the unheard melodies—inherent in ordinary prose. As she remarked, quite prosaically, in her 1924 version of "Poetry," "case after case / could be cited" to prove that so far as poetry is concerned, it isn't "valid / to discriminate against 'business documents and // school books'" since "all these phenomena are important" (*Complete Poems*, 267).

II.

"To break the pentameter": for Ezra Pound, that was the imperative task of Modern poetry (*Cantos* LXXI). Wordsworth contributed much to the effort, but so did a very different Romantic poet, Byron, whom Wordsworth despised. Though not so directly influenced by the British Elocutionary Movement as Wordsworth, his work is even more obviously grounded in oral and prose models and the falling rhythms of the English mother tongue. But unlike Wordsworth, he does not characteristically deploy an "overheard" style. He is a rhetorical poet, cultivating a direct reader address that ranges from an engaging conversational style to a high oratorical posture, with a remarkable range of interme-diate expressive modes. The second person, singular and plural, is ever present, often explicitly so. Nor is "conversational facility" (*Don Juan* XV.20) by any means confined to his late ottava rima masterpieces.[25] He is constantly talking to readers, or introducing characters in conversation, or—one his most arresting moves—mimicking different kinds of spoken and literary usage: Laura talking *at* Beppo just come back, unexpectedly and not entirely conveniently, to Venice (*Beppo* XCI–XCIII); Eve cursing her son Cain (III.1.443); Saint Peter and the angels Michael and Lucifer in polite conversation (*Vision of Judgment*); Julia haranguing her suspicious husband or, in an entirely different key, writing her farewell letter to Juan (*Don Juan* I.142–57, 192–97).

Don Juan is a poem that imagines English as a world language. It exploits multiple British dialects—sophisticated and vulgar, English and Scots—as well as multiple foreign languages, ancient and modern. It's pertinent to recall that no other Romantic poet undertook such an array of translation projects in multiple languages, ancient and modern, or executed so many parodies and pastiche renderings of linguistic and genre forms. This constant attention to English as a vernacular mash-up drives his intense interest in all types of communication, not just language. The entire lexicon and grammar of a polyglot English, hauling along with it the Western literary canon, seems far less a burden of the past laid on him than a library and toolkit put at his disposal.

Perhaps the most spectacular and informative example of Byron's situation comes in canto XI of *Don Juan* when he brings Juan "home" to England. At that point we recognize the source of his decisive insight into English prosody: his lexicon. None of his contemporaries, and no previous English poets other than Chaucer and Shakespeare, cultivate such a linguistic range. Juan's run-in with the highwayman Tom is explicitly cast as an English lesson (XI.12) that takes its examples from a low vulgate and, famously, flash slang. Told to stand and deliver—"Damn your eyes! Your money or your life!" (XI.10)—Juan is shaken from his reverie on English virtues:

> Juan yet quickly understood their gesture.
>   And being somewhat choleric and sudden,
> Drew forth a pocket pistol from his vesture,
>   And fired it into one assailant's pudding—
> Who fell, as rolls an ox o'er in his pasture,
>   And roared out, as he writhed his native mud in,
> Unto his nearest follower or henchman,
> "Oh Jack! I'm floored by that ere bloody Frenchman!"
>   (XI.13)

As the opening line's dactylic/trochaic rhythm openly declares, the law of the iamb has been expelled from the passage, its rhythms being admitted as occasion suggests. Elsewhere, multiple cadences on offer are not pentametrically or iambically shaped because they are transacted through the unheard syllabic rhythms of Italian ottava rima. That "soft bastard latin" (*Beppo* XLIV) frees Byron to shift his and our view of English, to see that it is indeed "made up of . . . all kinds of measures." To exploit them requires a decorum not based in a theory of styles but in a broad and sympathetic experience with English usage. Briefly, through as large a dictionary as possible. That would be a dictionary organized, like Murray's to come, "on historical principles," preserving all the language's noble living and noble dead and open to words unimagined yet in prose or rhyme.

As to that last point, another example from *Don Juan* comes immediately to mind: the pharmacological stanza in canto ten (see figure 1.4).

One of the best commentators on the passage, Peter Cochran, has said that its "problem has always been how are [the lines] to be read aloud."[26] But more is at stake here than recitation, though recitation—and linguistic *parole*—is an issue being provocatively raised. A brief detour into the contemporary poetic scene will be helpful at this point.

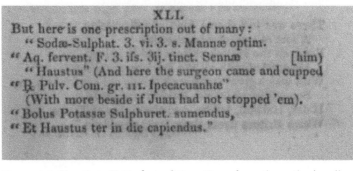

Figure 1.4. *Don Juan* X.41, first edition. Copy from the author's collection, on deposit in Special Collections, University of Virginia library, which supplied the image.

In a brilliant recent exhibition at the Getty Center's Research Institute—*Concrete Poetry: Words and Sounds in Graphic Space*—Nancy Perloff, the curator, called attention to the importance of sound for a poetic genre one often thinks has no relation to it.[27] But because concrete poems deal in elementary forms of language—letters, graphic marks, and the manifold ways they can be expressively arranged—they are often eloquent witnesses to the basic sounds that make sense *sensible*. Ian Hamilton Finlay's 1968 poem "Sea Poppy 2 (Fishing Boat Names)" is a concrete poem with an ambitious, virtually Neoplatonic display of the magical gesture involved in giving names to fishing boats (see figure 1.5).

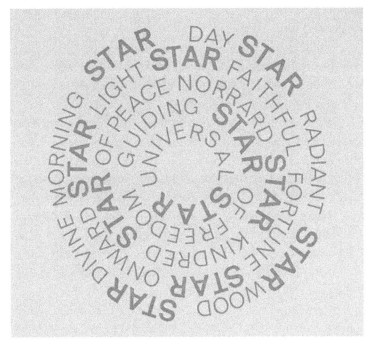

Figure 1.5. Ian Hamilton Finlay, "Sea Poppy 2 (Fishing Boat Names)" (1968). Black and white author's photograph of his copy of the commercial print, with blue background removed.

In a startling move, Perloff supplied a number of the exhibits with audio versions. "Sea Poppy 2 (Fishing Boat Names)" came with an audio recitation by Mark Tweddle. Perloff's curatorial decision was forecast in the book she had just published, *Explodity*. Subtitled *Sound, Image, and Word in Russian Futurist Book Art*, Perloff's study drew the important connection between that early twentieth-century futurist work (Malevich, Kruchenykh, Larionov) and later concrete and conceptual poetry.

Kruchenykh's sound poems, which created visual settings that would put "the sound as such" on graphic display, may seem far indeed from Wordsworth's and Coleridge's language experiments.[28] But they are not that far from Thelwall's or Hopkins's, and Byron's pharmacological stanza closes the gap even more, showing what becomes possible when verse expression is being reconceived root and branch.

Although all poetry, including concrete poetry, can and should be recited, some poems or parts of poems are better seen and not heard—a condition nicely exposed by a move to recite. *Don Juan* has several examples of this (see figure 1.6).

We're looking at how Byron's first and friendliest critics, his publisher and close friends, read these passages.[29] Perhaps they thought they were doing him a favor, expurgating lines that the public might not like. Whatever, Byron was furious at the intrusion and later editors, myself included, have restored all the passages asterisked in the first edition. But it's not difficult to see their erasure as a proper response, in several senses, to Byron's provocative call out. That defaced face value sets out a more than satisfying reading since it actually includes a reading of the poem in the poem.

And then notice the pencil cancellation of CXXX, another sign of an intruding reader. Who did that, and why? Kate McMasters and Alfred A. Johnston both owned the book before it came into the library of Duke University in 1923. Is the cancellation meaning to cancel what Byron's publisher and friends had done?

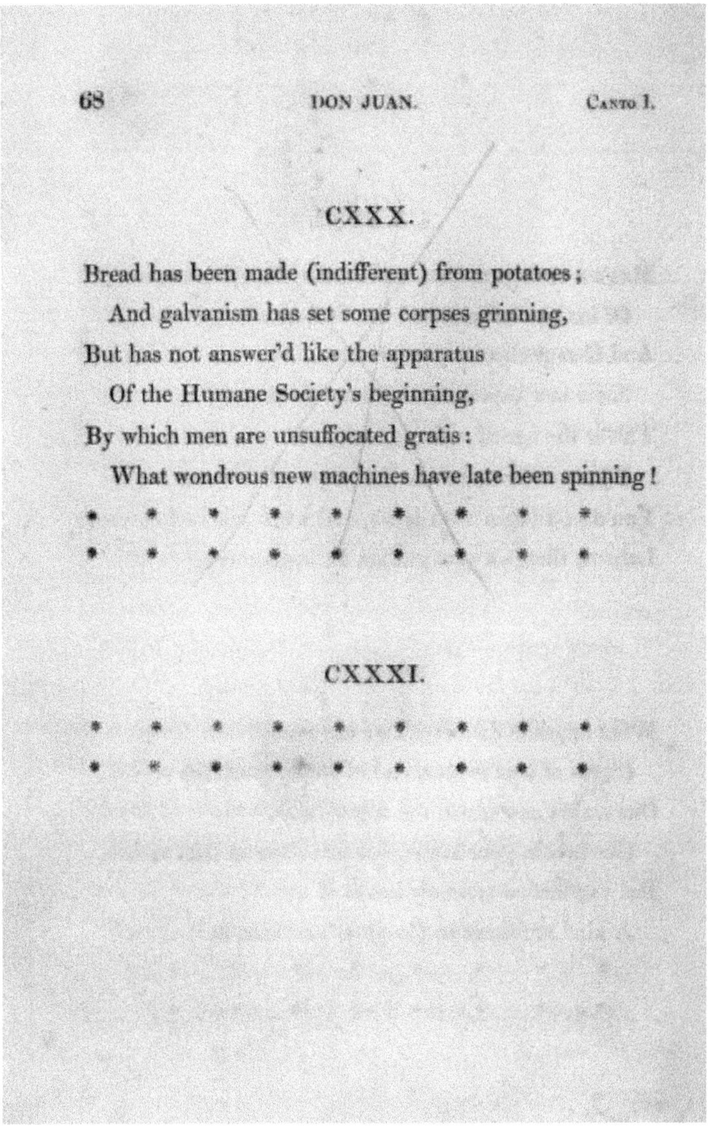

CXXX.

Bread has been made (indifferent) from potatoes ;
   And galvanism has set some corpses grinning,
But has not answer'd like the apparatus
   Of the Humane Society's beginning,
By which men are unsuffocated gratis :
   What wondrous new machines have late been spinning !

*   *   *   *   *   *   *   *   *
*   *   *   *   *   *   *   *   *

CXXXI.

*   *   *   *   *   *   *   *   *
*   *   *   *   *   *   *   *   *

Figure 1.6. Image of Canto I, stanzas 130–31, first edition, second issue of the 1819 edition of *Don Juan* in Duke University's Special Collections. Image in the public domain, Internet Archive, https://archive.org/details/donjuan03byro/page/68/mode/2up.

Apparently the work of either McMasters or Johnston, it is another instruction for reading. "Perfect freedom" is the name of this poetic game and it is definitely a multiplayer game.

III.

At the turn of the present century the digital humanities scholar Susan Hockey wrote about the effect that electronic textualities were having on our understanding of language as such. One comment was especially profound: "There is," she wrote, "no obvious unit of language."[30] The observation could be a summary reflection on the dramatic innovations in poetry and poetics that have taken place over the past 250 years. If any feature of language taken at any level can serve as the measure for its structure, there is no obvious limit to how rhythmic recurrence may be imagined and executed.

To demonstrate this, I close with a glance at Ron Silliman's discussion of what he called "The New Sentence."[31] The project examines the opportunities for prose poetry when "grammar has become . . . prosody" ("The New Sentence," 571). Silliman is aiming "to incorporate all the elements of language [into the prosody], from below the sentence level [phrases, words, letters] *and* above [the paragraph and sequence of paragraphs]" (575). Briefly, "the paragraph is a unit of quantity, not logic or argument," and "sentence length is a unit of measure," so that "the limiting of syllogistic movement keeps the reader's attention at or very close to the level of language, that is, most often at the sentence level or below" (574). Because he considers sub- and super-sentential elements only in terms of grammar, as if a sentence's grammar comprehended all its expressive elements, one might demur from his proposal. But his own discussion of prose poetries and exemplary new sentences shows that in practice these complexities of lexis, usage, and phonology have actually been assumed in what he calls "grammar."

Like Hockey's unobvious unit of language, Silliman's study of prose poetry has a greatly useful unintended consequence. It seems to me beyond question that the structuring order Silliman sees in New Sentence poetry is a regular feature of Byron's verse, whereas Wordsworth practices what Silliman would see as a proto-surrealist poetics, "manipulat[ing] meaning . . . at the higher or outer layers well beyond the level of the sentence" ("The New Sentence," 570). It is the difference Wallace Stevens captured in his famous distinction between "the beauty of inflections" and "the beauty of innuendoes" ("Thirteen Ways of Looking at a Blackbird")—a formulation, be it noted, that is thinking, as Wordsworth and Byron were thinking—of poetry in relation to *parole*.[32] Byron's verse regularly "keeps the reader's attention at or very close to" what is immediate and "uppermost, without delay" (*Don Juan* XIV.7). "Because, just as the stanza likes to make it, / It needs must be" (*Beppo* LXIII), the "story slips for ever through my fingers." It is far less the story than the story*telling* that matters. Indeed, the story is simply an excuse "to hook my rambling verse on" (*Beppo* LII).

So let me leave you with a glimpse of Byron's muse, appropriately named Laura, welcoming back her wandering husband in a style Byron called "that there sort of writing."[33] Here is a passage of New Sentence prosody in Regency vernacular exploiting the resources of ottava rima, especially caesura, lineation, and rhyme:

> "And are you *really, truly,* now a Turk?
>> With any other women did you wive?
> Is't true they use their fingers for a fork?
>> Well, that's the prettiest Shawl—as I'm alive!
> You'll give it me? They say you eat no pork.
>> And how so many years did you contrive
> To—Bless me! did I ever? No, I never
> Saw a man grown so yellow! How's your liver?"
>> (*Beppo* XCII)

Notes

1. Charles O. Hartman, *Free Verse: An Essay on Prosody* (Princeton, NJ: Princeton University Press, 1980), 12.

2. Paul Valéry, *Degas Manet Morisot*, trans. David Paul with an introduction by Douglas Cooper, Bollingen Series XLV:12 (Princeton, NJ: Princeton University Press, 1989), 62. For a good introduction to the poetics of orality, both as composition and as interpretation, see Anna Eyre's "Jaime de Angulo's Relational 'I': A Morphological Poetics," *Paideuma* 41 (2014): 79–110.

3. Stephen Gill, ed., *William Wordsworth*, Oxford Authors (New York: Oxford University Press, 1984), 602. Cited hereafter as Gill.

4. Samuel Taylor Coleridge, *Biographia Literaria*, ed. James Engell and W. Jackson Bate (Princeton, NJ: Princeton University Press, 1983), II:73.

5. See Wordsworth's reference to Hazlitt's preoccupation with "modern books of moral philosophy" in the "Advertisement" to the 1798 *Lyrical Ballads* and "The Tables Turned" (Gill, 130, 592).

6. The threat had been building for more than a century. Dryden's *Of Dramatic Poesy* (1666) pivots on the issues at stake, which go to the heart of the vigorous Ancients versus Moderns quarrel that carried forward into the Augustan period. For the Peacock quotation see *Peacock's Four Ages of Poetry; Shelley's Defence of Poetry; Browning's Essay on Shelley*, ed. H. F. B. Brett-Smith (Boston: Houghton Mifflin, 1921), 16.

7. John Thelwall, *Illustrations of English Rhythmus* (London: McCreery, 1812), xxi. Hereafter cited as *Illustrations*. See also his *Selections for the illustration of a course of instructions on the rhythmus and utterance of the English language . . .* , also published by McCreery in 1812.Thelwall is saying pretty much exactly what Ezra Pound would later argue in his *Antheil and the Treatise on Harmony* (Paris: Three Mountains Press, 1924): "I believe in an absolute rhythm" (13).

8. That is of course the context for Wordsworth's denunciation in his "Preface" of "frantic novels, sickly and stupid German Tragedies, and deluges of idle and extravagant stories in verse" (Gill, 599).

9. Williams's book-length study *The Embodiment of Knowledge*, written in 1928–1930, was only published posthumously (ed. Ron Loewinsohn, New York: New Directions, 1974).

10. The letter to Thelwall was written mid-January 1804. See *The Letters of William and Dorothy Wordsworth: The Early Years 1787–1805*,

ed. Ernest De Selincourt, 2nd ed., revised by Chester L. Shaver (Oxford: Oxford University Press, 1967), 431–35, 434. Hereafter cited as *Letters*. All the quotations from Wordsworth's letter below are to this text. Brennan O'Donnell discusses the letter at length in *The Passion of Meter: A Study of Wordsworth's Metrical Art* (Kent, OH: Kent State University Press, 1995), 26–33; see also Ruth Abbott's discussion, which follows O'Donnell, in her essay "Wordsworth's Prosody" in *The Oxford Handbook of William Wordsworth*, ed. Richard Gravil and Daniel Robinson (Oxford: Oxford University Press, 2015), 526–29.

11. Judith Thompson describes the context of the exchange of letters in 1804—that is, the controversy that Thelwall was having—and that Wordsworth encouraged—with the *Edinburgh Review* attack on both the *Lyrical Ballads*, Southey's *Thalaba the Destroyer* (1801), and Thelwall's *Poems, Chiefly Written in Retirement* (1801). See Judith Thompson, *John Thelwall in the Wordsworth Circle: The Silenced Partner* (New York: Palgrave Macmillan, 2012), 161–69, which greatly improves upon the note to the letter in the Oxford edition of the Wordsworth letters (*Letters*, 431n).

12. Nineteenth-century prosodists like Coventry Patmore responded to this feature of poetry with theories of verse "dipody," or two-footedness: lines that could be scanned and pronounced according to (at least) two different standard measures.

13. In his letter to John Hamilton Reynolds of September 22, 1819. Maurice Buxton Forman, ed., *The Letters of John Keats*, complete rev. ed. (London: Reeves & Turner, 1895), 380. The letter is especially striking because Keats is talking about his struggle in *Hyperion* with the legacy of Milton's literary language.

14. See Gill, 611.

15. John Thelwall, *A Letter to Henry Cline* (London: Taylor, 1810), 165.

16. *Letters*, 434.

17. Samuel Johnson, *Lives of the Poets*, new ed. (London: Kegan Paul, Trench, Trübner & Co., 1896), I:202.

18. *The Simple Wordsworth* (New York: Barnes & Noble, 1960) is the title—lifted from Byron's *English Bards and Scotch Reviewers*—of John Danby's fine study of the unpretentious lyric verse.

19. I allude to Donald Davie's important work on Romantic style, especially in his great study *Articulate Energy: An Inquiry into the Syntax of English Poetry* (London: Routledge and Kegan Paul, 1976). The quotation is from Laura Riding Jackson's *The Telling* (New York: Harper and Row, 1972), 66–67.

20. See Vincent A. de Luca, "A Wall of Words: The Sublime as Text," in *Unnam'd Forms: Blake and Textuality*, ed. Nelson Hilton and Thomas A. Vogler, 218–41 (Berkeley: University of California Press, 1986).

21. This is only one of the several similar raids that Whitman carried out upon his 1855 "Preface." All Whitman citations are to the texts provided online through *The Walt Whitman Archive*: https://whitmanarchive.org.

22. My texts for Moore come from Robin Schulze's superb critical edition *Becoming Marianne Moore: Early Poems 1907–1924* (Berkeley and Los Angeles: University of California Press, 2002); see especially 85–86 and 234–35. When necessary, I supplement with *Marianne Moore: The Complete Poems* (New York: Macmillan Company, Viking Press, 1967). Here see *Complete Poems*, 36. The 1918 text below is from *The Egoist* (August 1918): 95; the 1919 text below is from *Others for 1919: An Anthology of the New Verse*, ed. Alfred Kreyborg (New York: Nicholas Brown, 1920), 125–27.

23. A large decorative capital in *The Egoist* printing forced an indentation of lines 2–3.

24. Although Moore introduced a slight variation in the text to accommodate the new syllabic organization, the change does not affect the poem's basic prose rhythm.

25. My quotations from Byron's verse are from *Lord Byron: The Complete Poetical Works*, ed. Jerome McGann, 7 vols. (Oxford: Clarendon Press, 1983–1992). Citations are inline to line and/or stanza number.

26. Elaborating on Frank Stiling and Bruno Meinecke's *Explicator* essay, "Byron's DON JUAN, X, xli" (March 1949, article 36), Peter Cochrane has expended more effort to explicate the stanza than any previous scholar. See https://petercochran.files.wordpress.com/2009/03/don_juan_canto_10.pdf.

27. The exhibition, which ran from March 28–July 30, 2017, was an important follow-up to Perloff's *Explodity: Sound, Image, and Word in Russian Futurist Book Art* (Los Angeles: Getty Institute Research Publications, 2016).

28. Ibid., 72.

29. See as well in Canto I, stanzas 15 and 129 for other instances where Byron's publisher expurgated his text without Byron's knowledge, and—as here—supplied asterisks.

30. Susan Hockey, *Electronic Texts in the Humanities* (New York and Oxford: Oxford University Press, 2000), 20.

31. I quote from the cut and revised version he published in his anthology *In the American Tree* (Orono, ME: National Poetry Foundation, 1986), 561–75, where the central theoretical ideas and examples are given. Hereafter cited as "The New Sentence." The essay and several related essays were also published in Silliman's collection *The New Sentence* (New York: Roof Books, 1987), and this text is available online: http://writing.upenn.edu/library/Silliman-Ron_The-New-Sentence.pdf. That much looser 1987 essay is useful and interesting in a number of ways, however, not least in exposing how sharply Silliman's ideas have always been shaped by Saussure's distinction between *langue* (language, abstractly considered) and *parole* (speech). In his discussion of prose poetry, Silliman does not investigate "visible language"—its forms of representation in manuscript and print. Those forms might or might not reflect *parole*. But because, as Yeats observed, so much modern poetry—not least of all free verse and prose poetry—was born in the printing house, the visible deployments of expression are crucial features of all literary work, poetry as well as business documents.

32. In his useful study of *The American Prose Poem: Poetic Form and the Boundaries of Genre* (Gainesville: University Press of Florida, 1998), Michel Delville concludes that "the two main competing camps in the recent history of the prose poem in English" are what Silliman calls the Surrealist line and the New Sentence line (248).

33. *Byron's Letters and Journals,* ed. Leslie A. Marchand (Cambridge, MA: Harvard University Press, 1973–1982), 6:232.

Chapter 2

"My speech for that unspoken": Recitation and Recognition in T. S. Eliot's "Marina"

Response to Jerome McGann

Nikolaus Wasmoen

"*Quis hic locus, quae regio, quae mundi plaga?*"[1] T. S. Eliot drew these lines from Seneca's *Hercules* as the epigraph to his 1930 "Marina," a poem for which, to borrow a phrase from Jerome McGann, "every effort at recitation, every failed performance, restores the passion of a subject that has no ending." Eliot's poem, like its Senecan epigram, is in a sense precisely about the restorative potential of a poetic language tuned to inevitable failure. The poem opens with this short speech from Seneca, in which Hercules voices these questions as he regains his wits enough to realize that he has just wrought destruction not on the gods and heavens against which he had thought he raged, but on his own wife and family, whose corpses he now sees all around him mingled with the lingering spirits of the dead. Eliot saw this as one extreme pole of the dramatic "recognition scene," focused on loss and death, whereas his source for the body of the poem in Shakespeare's *Pericles*—where the titular king finds himself suddenly reunited with his erstwhile long-lost daughter, Marina—provided the opposite pole, associated with renewal and life.[2] In each case, the recognition scene presents a situation in which we are invited to pay close attention to the way that these opening speeches in the epigram and the first stanza seem to be responding to something that has already happened, at least with reference to the underlying plots of Eliot's dramatic sources where Hercules has already wrought destruction and Pericles is already reunited with his daughter, while at the same time performing a much more ambiguous linguistic temporality as they quiver on the boundaries between blindness and recognition, memory and perception, innocence and experience.

Reciting such a poem requires one to make choices about how to interpret and manage this ambiguity, through the heightening or smoothing out of cadences, rhythms, rhymes, punctuation, typography, lineation, layout, and other features of syntax and grammar. This paper examines the process of enacting such choices in recitation through the framework of translation described by Roman Jakobson. Jakobson's terminology and concepts help to navigate the terrain of "Marina" and its poetics, while casting recitation as a decisive, if still unlimited and variable, mode of poetic interpretation that might be realized and reproduced for the future through another form of interpretive performance in the form of textual encoding, to which I will return in this paper's conclusion.

Recitation might be defined as a kind of translation between a set of received signs, let's say in the form of a printed text, and its performance in recitation, in the form of an utterance. Jakobson describes the interpretation of language more generally in terms of such a translation: "the meaning of any linguistic sign is its translation into some further, alternative sign, especially a sign 'in which it is more fully developed.'"[3] This leads to the notion of "metalinguistic" operations that allow for revision and redefinition over the course of time based on the fitness of a given language to the purposes to which its speakers might want to put it.[4] While Jakobson's structuration of the linguistic field is rooted within a discussion of the logical foundation for the "linguistic science" he is seeking to develop, the way that he imagines translation and the types of metalanguage that it helps to propagate in connection to both everyday language and literary, poetic, or other specialized forms of language provides an effective framework to describe how such "more fully developed" semiotic systems, in one way or another, not only explain and elaborate their source signals but actually change their course. If we can only speak about what we can speak about speaking, then it follows that we can only meaningfully recite a poem to the extent that we can marshal its metalinguistic context.

As McGann points out, however, when it comes to teaching poetry in the classroom, many students express a deeply held belief, or paranoia, which I have encountered myself many times: that the metalinguistic elements of the verses I have assigned are the "real story" or the mysterious master key to a poem's meaningfulness, and that one either "gets" those things not spelled out in the text itself through the intervention of some altruistic magi, such as a professor offering a crib sheet to *Four Quartets*, or, say, an editor providing an explanatory introduction to *The Giaour*, or that one must master them somehow independently *before* even starting to make sense of the words presented by a given text. To be fair, who would not look around for help or salvation when that first *Quis* hits the eye? Or, put from another angle, how might we realign these expectations in a way that would allow such a reader to go ahead and read the actual poem in front of them aloud until she can credibly reproduce it aurally? What would be gained from such a realignment?

Whether or not the wider practice of recitation could effect such a change in expectations on the part of readers, and what might be gained or lost thereby, it would be helpful to clarify that I have been treating here loosely the difference between translations that take place among different forms or registers within a given language, such as between English-language poetry and English-language literary criticism, and those that take place across distinct languages, such as English and Latin. These differences may not be quite as crucial in cases where we are speaking mostly about what readers *do not have* at their disposal to aid interpretation. For example, not knowing the English term *paronomasia* is not much different from not knowing the Latin word *paronomasia* or not knowing the Greek παρονομασία. The confluence of multiple languages in a poem, however, has the potential to bring metalinguistic features to greater awareness, perhaps most strongly in recitation when contrasts in syntax, grammar, and morphemes become audible.

For Jakobson, the difference between languages raises a series of imperative questions for a speaker, which I would argue hold even when that speaker is reciting language already written for them: "Languages differ essentially in what they *must* convey and not in what they *may* convey. Each verb of a given language imperatively raises a set of specific yes-or-no questions, as for instance: is the narrated event conceived with or without reference to its completion? Is the narrated event presented as prior to the speech event or not? Naturally the attention of native speakers and listeners will be constantly focused on such items as are compulsory in their verbal code."[5] During recitation these types of questions can make it hard to follow what one is reading as lines and sentences unfold and, especially in languages with scarce tense markers, a reader must decide between multiple, equally grammatically correct possibilities that may nonetheless be interpretively incompatible. In "Marina," the language of the poem's first line operates like a loose gloss of the epigraph, but with the significant change from the question form, "*Quis . . .*" to a more emphatic adjectival form, "What . . ." Like Ezra Pound, Eliot often glosses foreign language when it appears in the tissue of his verse. When Eliot translates his source, here, however, he treats the poetic utterance as if it were being produced by someone in a very similar situation and attitude as a reciter of the poem would find herself in: in these dramatic moments Hercules and Pericles are searching for the words to describe what they can only begin to recognize, while the reciter of "Marina" will need to make choices about how to parse its simple yet twisty opening.

As the reciter enters into this interpretive activity, she is estranged from everyday language, in which metalinguistic codes are rarely raised to awareness, and moved into a space where the rules of the language game become something more interactive, more capacious. In the case of the tragic epigraph to "Marina," the reader is literally asked to imagine this strangeness in spatial terms: "What place is this, what region, what tract of the earth?" begins the poem in a relatively straight translation into English.[6] The terms of the tragic hero's estrangement, as explained by Paul Hammond in *The Strangeness of Tragedy*, apply to the predicament of the interpreter of a poem in recitation:

> Hercules exemplifies a mode of estrangement . . . characteristic of tragedy, a movement of translation and of decomposition. The protagonist is translated out of his normal time and space into forms of these which others cannot inhabit. . . . The space in which he stands is one which has been transformed by his imagination into a terrain contoured by guilt or ambition or desire. . . . The time in which he moves is not the time of his neighbours, but a dimension in which what they would call the past is urgently present to him, or in which the future seems already to have happened; laws of sequence, of cause and effect, no longer apply. Language no longer joins the protagonist to his social milieu.[7]

As a poem that draws primarily from two dramatic sources, Seneca and Shakespeare, for both its language and subject, "Marina" forces its would-be reciter almost immediately to begin to make choices about the ways that they will translate the written word into speech. The first line of the poem provides a loose gloss of the epigraph:

> What seas what shores what grey rocks and what islands
> What water lapping the bow
> And scent of pine and the woodthrush singing through
>   the fog
> What images return
> O my daughter. (lines 1–5)

At first, this translation occurs between languages, but as the first sentence unfolds over the next four lines, it becomes clear that the poetry of "Marina" takes place not only in the translation of Latin into English, but also within different domains of English itself. When one begins to rehearse meticulously to recite a poem, the words become less fixed than they would be in everyday communication, where repetition is generally avoided rather than pursued. That odd feeling of having repeated a word or a line until it seems almost to have lost its meaning suggests an alienation from language as a social milieu that is not without parallel to the alienation of the tragic hero mulling her surroundings. One of the metalinguistic codes operating upon the meaning of Eliot's poem is indeed the generic expectations for tragic heroes. By reciting the poem, these codes can be not only revealed but exposed in action, allowing a reader to actively participate in their operation.[8] As such metalinguistic processes proliferate and as a reader becomes better at recognizing them in operation, the act of recitation will become a more and more powerful interpretive tool even as it becomes less and less predictable or repeatable. Each time a new fork in the decision tree enacted during a reading is opened, it multiplies the possible states of everything that will follow it, multiplying the complexity and subtlety of what one can do in terms of translating a poetic text into speech. After Romanticism, it should not be surprising that, like all tragic world-building, recitations, when considered as intersemiotic translations of words into sounds, are bound to fall short, to fail to exhaust their subjects, since in the differences between languages and semiotic systems a host of alternative possibilities will arise.[9]

The primary metalinguistic aid with which we have been equipped for recitation is the understanding of the relationship between poetic speech and common speech, the primary subject of McGann's exploration of the historical roots of his reflections on, and practices of, recitation. McGann traces the development in the Romantic period of competing notions about how much poetic speech ought, or ought not, to be performed in the manner of everyday speech, and to what extent one should force one's reading aloud, or composition in anticipation of being read aloud, to conform to given meters, usually iambic. The "law of the iamb" is the conventionalization of what sociolinguistic reformers such as John Thelwall put forth as the "abstract rhythmus" suffusing all of English, or poets such as Keats cast as "the true voice of feeling" according to McGann's account. What emerges is an understanding of recitation as a dynamic between "the passion of metre," specifically "the regular laws of iambic versification," and "the passion of the subject," the subjective interpretation of irregular and/or mixed meters that must be curbed to avoid confusion and inconsistency.

The notion of a passion of the subject can also be approached as a question of the extent to which poetic speech is required to submit to the syntactical and grammatical rules for English. Hugh Kenner argued that "Marina" is not organized syntactically at all like a statement, but instead "musically" in terms of a spatialized ordering:

> Some parts of "Marina" can be treated as sentences
> and some parts cannot. . . . One probably wants to
> call it "musical," based on associations and recur-
> rences, among them the Shakespearean associations
> aroused by the title. It is as far as Eliot ever went in
> that particular direction . . . : the poem faced toward
> a domain of waking dream, so certain of its diction
> that we concede it a coherence it need not find means
> of specifying. It has no paraphrasable structure at
> all, and yet seems to affirm its elusive substance as
> authoritatively as Mozart.[10]

To follow the musical logic of "Marina" in this argument is to
go "in that particular direction" and to face "toward a domain
of waking dream." Kenner describes Eliot here in terms similar
to those Hammond used to depict the tragic hero's estrangement
from the everyday language of her contemporaries. For example,
as previously discussed, the word *What* opens "Marina" not with
a question but as an adjective modifying a sequence of nouns:
"seas," "shores," "grey rocks," "islands," "water," and finally "What
images return / O my daughter." These are ostensibly the things
that Pericles sees from where he is located aboard a boat meeting
his daughter for the first time since he had come to believe she
was lost and gone forever. The verse is presenting a language
that belies a struggle with the oncoming rush of impressions that
Pericles and Marina's long-delayed reunion has precipitated. These
*what*s seem to answer the imperative questions facing Pericles at
that precise moment: what am I seeing, hearing, and experiencing?
Stunned and slowly inching toward recognition, Pericles is reduced
to cataloging the sensoria that surround him, but how should one
read the following sentence(s) of the poem that extends over the
next four stanzas, with two sets of terminal punctuation, first a
question mark and then a period, inconsistent capitalization, and
an array of syntactic shapeshiftings:

Those who sharpen the tooth of the dog, meaning
Death
Those who glitter with the glory of the humming-
    bird, meaning
Death
Those who sit in the stye of contentment, meaning
Death
Those who suffer the ecstasy of the animals, meaning
Death

Are become unsubstantial, reduced by a wind,
A breath of pine, and the woodsong fog
By this grace dissolved in place

What is this face, less clear and clearer
The pulse in the arm, less strong and stronger—
Given or lent? more distant than stars and nearer
    than the eye

Whispers and small laughter between leaves
    and hurrying feet
Under sleep, where all the waters meet. (lines 6–21)

The flood of recognition begins with a litany of various *Those*s
whose images mean death, but after the fourth exhortation to
Death a sudden redirection takes place across a stanza break,
as "a wind" emerges to dissolve this phantasmagoria, suddenly
"become unsubstantial." Pericles's recognition of his daughter is
rendered not as a singular revelation but instead as an outpouring
of barely assimilated recognitions firing in rapid sequence and tied
together by the strange speech of the hero in its starts and stops
and redirections. These lines culminate sequentially and syntactically in a compressed catalog of the poetic palette from which
these movements are built: haunting "whispers" and "laughter

between" intertextual "leaves," irregular poetic "feet" which pro-
pel the poem between "hurrying" and "sleep," and an abstracted
mental space "where all the" questions like those described with
reference to Jakobson arise, the w[h]aters lapping throughout the
poem accumulating together from its dreamlike point of view. The
general impression wrought by the poem seems, then, to involve
not only the translation of various sources or textual materials
from one language or form into another, but the translation of the
reader's perspective into something very much like the passion of
the tragic subjects who provide the poem its contrasting centers
of consciousness in *Hercules* and *Pericles*.

A reciter's imagination and reason exert their influence on her
interpretive performances of "Marina" aloud through the posing of
a great number of micro-recognitions. These micro-recognitions
can take place on any level, or number of levels, of the poem's
organization. McGann describes what amounts to a sense of freedom from poetic and typographic convention made possible by
the (most) "dramatic innovations in poetry and poetics" since the
1760s, those of Romanticism and Modernism. In brief, the ways
that these movements had cast off, successively and in combination,
the bonds of earlier metrical and typographic conventions for verse
opened the way for a subtler and more expansive understanding
of poetic language's overdetermined structures. Expanding on an
observation by Susan Hockey regarding the multitudinous ways
electronic texts can be organized and structured into corpora,
that "there is no obvious unit of language," McGann describes a
radically expanded field for the practice of poetic language: "If
any feature of language taken at any level can serve as the measure for its structure, there is no obvious limit to how rhythmic
recurrence may be imagined and executed." In Eliot's poem, this
sense of an opening up of language through the explosion of its
potential prosodic structurations is symbolized as a new depar-
ture from "This form, this face, this life" toward an experience
of "Living to live in a world of time beyond me" (lines 29–30).

At this point in the poem's penultimate stanza, Pericles speaks for only the second time as if he might be talking or referring to someone else, the first being his exclamation "O my daughter" in the first sentence.

> . . . let me
> Resign my life for this life, my speech for that unspoken,
> The awakened, lips parted, the hope, the new ships.
>   (lines 30–32)

The syntax of this language of "time beyond me" is fragmented and repetitive, but its mixed meters seem to open up a space in which the indeterminacy and variability of the flow and direction of this speech bespeak of hopeful potentials, "new ships" to go on new departures. The oneiric, litanous qualities of this halting but increasingly confident language are thrown into sharp relief by the reappearance in the next and final stanza of almost the same iambs with which the poem opened, "What seas what shores . . ." The final three-line stanza, however, compresses and adjusts even as it repeats much of the opening stanza, taking only eighteen words to reach "My daughter" instead of the thirty-two words required at the outset; for example, "what grey rocks and what islands" is distilled to "what granite islands" (line 33), which smooths the procession of *what*s. These compressions prepare us to hear "*My* daughter" (emphasis added) two lines later not only as the culmination of the progression of personal pronouns and possessives in the poem, its austerely distributed *me*s and *my*s, but also the sequence of protean adjectival *What*s that have been acting like the result of interpretive questions posed by the oncoming of partial, tangential recognitions leading up to the main crux of the poem: what Pericles is seeing and who he is talking to is simply the daughter he addresses, "My daughter," and no longer the metrical exigency of "O my daughter" under the sign of the law of the iamb, which has finally been broken.

Alertly and assiduously reading this poem aloud may ultimately only be one way, or one of a set of techniques, to unlock
the meanings encoded within its meter and rhythms. In conclusion, I would like to suggest that in addition to translation, we
might consider recitation as remediation, following Jay David
Bolter and Richard Grusin's use of this term at the end of the
last century in their study of the remediation of content and form
from established media to new media.[11] Remediation is similar in
some respects to what Jakobson described as intersemiotic translation, that is translation between discrete semiotic systems, but
with a different point of emphasis on the ways that audiovisual
and digital media attempt to recreate the effect of "immediacy"
for their users by mimicking or intensifying aspects of precursor
works in earlier media. These new media attempt "to achieve
immediacy by ignoring or denying the presence of the medium
and the act of mediation," such as in the examples of a "painting
by the seventeenth-century artist Pieter Saenredam, a photograph
by Edward Weston, and a computer system for virtual reality" that
all seek to realize this effect regardless of how different the ways
they might use to do so are.[12] In contrast to Jakobson's generally
media-agnostic discussion of language as a subject for scientific
analysis, Bolter and Grusin provide a useful terminology for
describing our constant movement between multiple overlapping
mediums as a product of a desire to form alternative temporal
relationships to the content we seek. It is worth taking notice as a
reader of the medium or media through which the linguistic signs
of a beloved poem are delivered to you, and to question how the
immediacy offered by some versions may or may not serve the
subtle play of meter and temporal expansion and dilation traced
through the practice of recitation. Doing so, we might remark
upon the lack of much of an embedded record on the printed
page of Eliot's poem of any of the finer points of prosody with
which we have been treating. If prosodic analysis is to be passed
on to the future, not only its content but also its lively practice,

it would seem to need to be remediated digitally in a way that will ensure we can recreate it without forestalling the inevitable failure of any recitation or scansion to exhaust the passion of the subject in poetry. A technique is required that will afford both multiplicity in interpretation and attention to the forces and effects of digital mediation as our artistic and cultural heritage inevitably moves further online.

Along these lines, we might turn to textual encoding and markup as a means toward the reproducibility of poetic meters and recitation data. For example, using XML (Extensible Markup Language) or other metadata formats it becomes possible to separate the base text from the various non-alphanumeric information that alters our interpretation of so-called "plain text," which is of course never really "plain" but instead always modified by fonts, typography, layout, physical or visual states, associations with other objects, and by its context on the screen or page or disk. The ability to separate out these kinds of textual metadata from textual contents enables us in turn to record more abstract and critical information about a text, without distorting or overwriting the given fact of the textual artifact or the signs inscribed on it. We could, for example, encode the similar opening and closing stanzas of "Marina" as distinct stanzas as these occur in the printed ordering of the poem—as well as any variants we might identify among the available textual witnesses to the poem—as well as, and at the same time, variations of a single stanza, or as separate instantiations of a shared model of a stanza that is incompletely realized in either case. The possibilities are manifold, but, as McGann has helped to clarify as much as anyone within our current discourse about the fate of poetry, and arts and letters more broadly, the stakes are high.

Both recitation and textual encoding serve to remove our experiences of poetry from the pressure of, and the pressure to achieve, the kind of unscrupulous, blinkered immediacy that has been bequeathed to us by Web 2.0, social media ubiquity, and other subsequently intensifying factors that make the promise of a more sustainable and productive relationship to the time we spend inhabiting creative works only seem more urgent and appealing. To grow and foster those kinds of relationships to our poetic heritage, we must be willing to act decisively and thoughtfully at the same time in our interpretations. While practices such as recitation and textual encoding are only bound by the amount of thinking, looking, speaking, and typing that we are willing or able to engage in to produce them, these forms of engagement with poetry require us to make our judgments and choices explicit in our interpretive performance of a text. We can have in either recitation or encoding multiple well-articulated and supported interpretations of the same poem or passage, but we must be willing to make those critical wagers in full knowledge that these will but provide the scaffolding for future performances as our poetry continues to be adjusted by, and comes to adjust, the course of our language'(s') future histories.[13] Let us go then, "towards my timbers / And woodthrush calling through the fog" (lines 33–34) after what we are told Byron called "that there sort of writing," and when we find it, let us make sure to pass it on as caringly as those who have made it available to us.

Notes

1. T. S. Eliot, "Marina," *Complete Poems and Plays 1909–1950* (New York: Harcourt, Brace & World, 1971), 72–73.

2. Eliot wrote to Sir Michael Sadler to explain this intention on May 9, 1930: "I intend [in "Marina"] a criss-cross between Pericles finding alive, and Hercules finding dead—the two extremes of the recognition scene." Quoted in Richard Abel, "The Influence of St.-John Perse on T. S. Eliot," *Contemporary Literature* 14, no. 2 (Spring 1973): 235n52.

3. Roman Jakobson, "On Linguistic Aspects of Translation," in *On Translation*, ed. Reuben A. Brower (Cambridge, MA: Harvard University Press, 1959), 233; the embedded quotation, "in which it is more fully developed," is from Charles Sanders Peirce and is reprinted in *Collected*

Papers of Charles Sanders Peirce, vol. 5, eds. Charles Hartshorne and Paul Weiss (Cambridge, MA: Harvard University Press, 1934): "But a sign is not a sign unless it translates itself into another sign in which it is more fully developed. Thought requires achievement for its own development, and without this development it is nothing. Thought must live and grow in incessant new and higher translations, or it proves itself not to be genuine thought" (594).

4. Jakobson: "A faculty of speaking a given language implies a faculty of talking about this language" (ibid., 234).

5. Ibid., 236.

6. Translation from Paul Hammond, *The Strangeness of Tragedy* (Oxford/New York: Oxford University Press, 2009), 3.

7. Ibid.

8. In Marianne Moore's contemporary review of "Marina," published as "A Machinery of Satisfaction," *Poetry* 38, no. 6 (September 1931): 337–39, she describes the reader sharing with the author a "machinery of satisfaction": "T. S. Eliot is occupied with essence and instrument. . . . Not sumptuous grossness but a burnished hedonism is renounced. Those who naively proffer consolation put the author beyond their reach, in initiate solitude. Although solitude is to T. S. Eliot, we infer, not 'a monarchy of death,' each has his private desperations; a poem may mean one thing to the author and another to the reader. What matters here is that we have, for both author and reader, a machinery of satisfaction that is powerfully affecting, intrinsically and by association. The method is a main part of the pleasure: lean cartography; reiteration with compactness; emphasis by word pattern rather than by punctuation; the conjoining of opposites to produce irony; a counterfeiting verbally of the systole, diastole, of sensation—of what the eye sees and the mind feels; the movement within the movement of differentiated kindred sounds" (338).

9. I do not mean to imply that there are not inaccurate or imprecise ways to recite verse, only that by conceiving of the interpretation of a poem in recitation as a series of choices to be made, a poem of any length or complexity will present an almost infinite series of interpretive outcomes arrayed like dynamically branching trees.

10. Hugh Kenner, *Historical Fictions* (Atlanta: University of Georgia Press, 1990), 164; quoted and discussed in Denis Donaghue, "Eliot's 'Marina' and Closure," *Hudson Review* 49, no. 3 (Autumn 1996): 367–88.

11. Jay David Bolter and Richard Grusin, *Remediation: Understanding New Media* (Cambridge, MA: MIT Press, 1999).

12. Ibid., 11.

13. See also Geoffrey H. Hartman, *Saving the Text: Literature/ Derrida/Philosophy* (Baltimore and London: John Hopkins University Press, 1981): "Emily Dickinson could call her poems 'my letter to the world'; so the literary text or artifact is a gift for which the interpreter must find words, both to recognize the gift, and then to allow it to create a reciprocating dialogue, one that might overcome the embarrassment inspired by art's riddling strength" (135–36).

Chapter 3

Jerome McGann's "Reading (I Mean Articulating) Poetry, a Multiplayer Game"

A Response

STEVE MCCAFFERY

Let me start by openly admiring the sustained brilliance of McGann's argument and making clear that this response is deliberately discontinuous and only addresses aspects and part-aspects of the talk that grasped my interest. The majority of my responses relate to the historical trajectory of his paper and the consequent omissions of what I consider important points. In conclusion I offer alternative engagement to recitation that is available from certain texts.

McGann: "My subject today is poetry and how my students do and don't deal with it."

McCaffery: Which brings up the important and contentious question: should the reading of poetry be an earned privilege? One should be wary of generalizing on this matter. To read, say, Williams's "The Red Wheelbarrow" is a radically different experience from reading Pope's *Rape of the Lock*, while an encounter with Skelton's "The Tunning of Eleanor Rumming" might remind students of rap and spoken word. Such "poetic" vocabulary as "eftsoons, methinks, welkin" is understandably alien to young contemporary minds, indicating the fact that language is in flux (an observation that goes back at least to Horace). The question, too, arises: are we in the midst of a revolution in reading language? In an ethos of social media and its character constraint, we are solidly in a world of what I will call "lipography," an abbreviatory imperative. OMG R U C ree S? Such orthographic reductions do not begin in the era of Twitter and texting. Indeed, the use of ligature and contractions was a common practice in Latin typography. Malcolm B. Parkes gives a splendid account of the picaresque narrative of the semicolon, first used as a punctuation mark in English texts in 1589 and earlier used as a ligature mark in Latin texts for the suffix *que*.[1] In the era of manual typesetting the compositor's rule emerged as a constant contingency (lack of space, lack of letter type, etc.) and opened a radical instability in the orthography of early texts.

McGann discusses Wordsworth's choice of the appropriate language for poetry. After quoting Wordsworth: "Prose [is the] natural or regular part of [a] language [so that] the language of every good poem can in no respect differ from that of good prose. We will go further. It may be safely affirmed, that there neither is, nor can be, any essential difference between the language of prose and metrical composition." McGann writes, "Perhaps no comment by an English poet has been more consequential than that. Reading it now we can hardly not think of the downstream watershed of free verse, prose poetry, and even concrete poetry."

McCaffery: The introduction of concrete poetry here requires some clarification and distinction. Concrete poetry emerged in the early 1950s (primarily in Europe and Brazil) as an intermedial practice whose texts (frequently nonlinear) fall formally between poetry and painting. The implications of this interstitial status articulate onto reception. A concrete poem is comprehended and interpreted via a mixed experience of seeing and reading. Its fundamental nonlinearity also radically alters the "time" of reading. For example, if we take Finlay's "Sea Poppy 2 (Fishing Boat Names)" included in the talk, the question arises: where do we start to read and for how long? Temporality becomes skewed because the poem elicits both lexical temporality (the time of reading) and pictorial temporality (how long do we look at a picture before all information and sensation is exhausted?). Eugen Gomringer, a founding practitioner, defined the "reader/reciter's" role in a "play-activity" (*denkgegenstanddenkspiel*) in which recitation (though possible) is a secondary concern.[2] Moreover, McGann's Wordsworthian watershed flows not only forward to concrete poetry but backwards to archaic anticipations. Though the product of a Cold War ethos, the poetics of concrete poetry enjoys a rich lineage going back through the *calligrammes* of Apollinaire, Addison's textual culprits of "false wit" (such as George Herbert's pattern poem "Easter Wings"), and the Roman *carmen figurata* back to the ancient Greek *technopaegnia*.

McGann: "But what brought Wordsworth to make his famous declaration? It turns out that the issue of poetic recitation was pivotal. When Wordsworth writes about 'the language of every good poem,' the language he has in mind is spoken, not literary, English. More, it is the spoken prose 'really used by men [in] low and rustic life.'"

McCaffery: As McGann implies but does not state outright, the issue of pronunciation becomes pivotal. Shelley and Keats, for instance, would have recited their poems with a Cockney accent and Tennyson with a Lincolnshire. In the latter's case, he also experimented with dialect as, for instance, in "The Northern

Farmer." I've always felt Wordsworth's division of his "common man" into rustic and industrial a grand testimony to an atavistic primitivism, a primitivism close to Emerson's that would privilege the rural and pastoral over the civic and industrial as being intuitively closer to "essential" nature. Homer functions as the eponym of this Romantic figure, the man spared the consequences of social contamination, the man closest to a pure relation with nature. Such primitivism hides a hygienic program that sees the path of so-called progress as a schedule toward corruption and mediation. Lurking but quite apparent in Wordsworth's "Preface" is his preserving of the rustic man from his industrial compatriots: the coal miner and glass worker, the mill worker and the laborer.

In his fascinating discussion of Thelwall, **McGann** writes: "A poet himself, Thelwall shared Wordsworth's and Coleridge's concerns about poetry and elevated forms of cultural practice. But he set those interests in a far more extensive social context. He became a community educator promoting language competence for everyone."

McCaffery: Alongside Thelwallian elocution we might consider the earlier interests in shorthand. I'm thinking especially of the Manchester poet John Byrom (1692–1763) who developed and taught a shorthand system taught to all classes and subsequently adopted officially by Oxford and Cambridge universities. The economic interest in scriptive brevity by means of non-romanic characters seems a persistent and beguiling bedfellow to pronunciation and connects, too, to the larger and more complex issue of cryptonomy.

McCaffery: I would only add to McGann's astute reading of the language of the Lucy poem a consideration of the apostrophe "oh" that occurs in the third line. As the young Hegel noted, what distinguishes vowels from consonants is the element of potential continuum that evades the discontinuity established by consonants. (Simply pronounce "eeee" as a continuum and "p"—not "p" pronounced "pee" which inserts the vowel continuum but as a plosive "puh"—to note the difference.) The question that arises in recitation is less how is this sound-word pronounced as when does it end?

McGann: "And then there is the astonishing *Laocoön* (c. 1826–1827), which is manifestly an instance of what we now call concrete poetry."

McCaffery: I find myself in disagreement with the claim that Blake's *Laocoön* "is manifestly an instance of what we now call concrete poetry." If it is, then so are the political cartoons of Blake's contemporary James Gillray. To my mind Blake's piece registers its affiliation with the political cartoon of the eighteenth century as it emerged in the work of Gillray and earlier in George, Marquis of Townshend. Townshend published a group of political cartoons in his *Political and Satyrical History of the Years 1756 and 1757*.[3] It is Townshend who introduced caricature into political print, and part of his innovation was the introduction of speech bubbles to convey a written text. It is known that in 1773 Blake bought a copy of the first edition. Again, as in McGann's watershed claim about Wordsworth, Blake is equally a Janusian figure looking forward to the intermedia texts of the twentieth century but equally back to the intermedia works of the mid-eighteenth century. Returning to the Blakean "wall of words" McGann includes in figure 1.3, it strikes me that its part origin within eighteenth-century cartoon semiology is not a farfetched notion, but rather one that is hard to dispute. The "wall of words" illustrated can be seen as a veritable speech balloon without a speaker. (It's also a well-known fact that Blake appropriated several of his images from designs on the faces of contemporary bank token coinage that circulated as a supplement to the regular currency of his day.)

McCaffery: Regarding McGann's discussion of Byron's *Don Juan*: As well as the pentametric pliancy that Byron masters there is the dazzling dexterity in his rhyme. One of the sheer delights in reading *Don Juan* is experiencing that phenomenon of the impossible rhyme made possible. A few samples from Canto V barely do justice to Byron's sonic acrobatics: "pukes in / Euxine," "for Pyramus / Semiramis," "Courier / jury here," "apartment / What art meant." It is as if Byron is testing the limits of rhyme, straining to a maximum that constraint and registering it as a grand athleticism.

In terms of the genealogy of *Don Juan*, mention should also be made of John Hookham Frere's *Prospectus and Specimen of an Intended National Work* to which Byron was indebted for the form of *Beppo*.[4] E. H. Coleridge claims (in his edition of *Don Juan*) that Frere led Byron into the study of the Italian ottava rima poets, like Pulci, Berni, and Ariosto.

McGann: "Kruchenykh's sound poems, which created visual settings that would put 'the sound as such' on graphic display, may seem far indeed from Wordsworth's and Coleridge's language experiments. But they are not that far from Thelwall's or Hopkins's, and Byron's pharmacological stanza closes the gap even more, showing what becomes possible when verse expression is being reconceived root and branch."

McCaffery: With the advent of the two Futurisms (Italian and Russian) we find the poem being radically reconsidered as score. Aided by the advances in commercial typography, the poem is granted a new status as notation. McGann mentions exclusively Russian developments, but a more entire picture must include the Dada *lautgedicht* and the Italian Marinetti's historically important

"Technological Manifesto for Futurist Literature" for "words in freedom."[5] The Dadaist Raoul Hausmann outlines a principle of "optophonetic" notation that facilitates variations in tone and volume by means of a type size correlation (small font rendered as soft sound, large font as loud). A large variety of types is deployed in one printed version of Ball's poem "Karawane" that deploys a different font for each of its seventeen lines, and a similar exploitation of visual notation along optophonetic lines can be noted in several of the *canone rumorista* or noise poems of the Italian Futurists.

McCaffery: As for McGann on the New Sentence: It may be taken as a point of irony that the essay closes with a short discussion of the New Sentence. Reflecting on the vanguard trajectory of the twentieth century, we can read the entirety of its literary inventions as delineating the changing destiny for the sentence. From its entire abolition in the poetics of *parole in libertá*, through its restitution in Surrealist texts (automatic writing always produces sentences), to its contested status among the Language poets. I think here of the phrasal units in extreme disjunction that characterize much of Bruce Andrews's work and the deployment of the phrase, rather than the sentence, as the governing poetic unit in my own work *Lag* and the early work of Karen Mac Cormack (to give two pertinent non-American examples.)

McCaffery: To return to the broad topic of recitation. McGann does not discuss one alternative to recitation: performance. I have in mind much of the poetry of Jackson Mac Low, especially the multivoice performance scores of the Gathas, multilinear texts inscribed on quadrilateral paper that offer the reader a multiplicity of reading paths and enunciatory choices. Such texts emancipate "recitation" from both pedagogy and hermeneutic interpretation. In the Gathas, one enters the score as a network of performative possibilities and necessary encounters. Moreover, the multiple vocalization of such texts opens up the non-scriptive and sigilistic domains of listening, pause, and silence. Understanding in this way the poem as a schema for the construction of community makes ineluctable the inflexion of ethics as indisputable and beyond innuendo.

Notes

1. M. B. Parkes, *Pause and Effect: An Introduction to the History of Punctuation in the West* (Berkeley: University of California Press, 1993).

2. Eugen Gomringer, "From Line to Constellation," *Artes Hispanica* 1, no. 3/4 (Winter & Spring 1968): 67.

3. George, Marquis of Townshend, *Political and Satyrical History of the Years 1756 and 1757* (London: E. Morris, 1759).

4. Both titles were published in London by John Murray in 1818.

5. F. T. Marinetti, *Selected Writings,* ed. R. W. Flint (New York: Farrar, Straus and Giroux, 1971), 84–89.

PART II

Chapter 4

2018 Robert Creeley Lecture in Poetry and Poetics: *Dous Chantar*

Refrain for a Nightingale

LISA ROBERTSON

The severed tongue lies palpitating on the dark earth, faintly murmuring.

—Ovid, *Metamorphoses*

When birds sing in early troubadour poems, they sing in lat-in—"en lor lati" as William IX, Duke of Aquitaine, Count of Poitiers (1071–1127), wrote in the Occitan language in his poem beginning with the line "Ab la dolchor del temps novel": "In the sweetness of the new season / the woods leaf out and each bird / sings in its latin."[1] *Lati,* latin, was the medieval Occitan word for anybody's specific speech. The presence of birds—via birdsong and also bird speech, where song and speech seem undifferentiated—is a commonplace in these first authored vernacular poems on the European continent. Starlings, nightingales, swallows, crows, magpies act as messengers, moving discretely between the poet and the beloved and back, or they are announcers of the turn of winter to spring, of the coming of love and leaf. They're in dialogue with poets. For poets and birds, as the season or the time is new, as William IX of Aquitaine's verse repeats, so is song, speech, desire. This newness is an effect of the surprise of temporal difference in repetition expressed so vividly by means of the then-innovative compositional technique called rime,[2] and it was an intensely debated theological and aesthetic problem about the origins of divine and human creation. Is newness made from nothing? (William IX began another poem, "I will make a verse of exactly nothing / There'll be nothing in it about me or anybody else."[3]) How do we explain the quivering in what seems the same? Or is new composition a rearrangement of existing parts? How did God make the Earth, and from what? And how is a new poem made by its author? How much of innovation is citational? These medieval questions are contemporary in their relevance. The quality called "newness" or "innovation," still a core value and problem within contemporary avant-gardes, also inaugurated that earlier avant-garde secular verse culture, the one called "troubadour." In the eleventh century, the new poetry announces itself in community with birds, who themselves sing, claims William IX in his poem "Segon lo vers de novel chan" ("On the model of the new rime," my translation). Poets and birds learn from one another, take one another as masters.

In the classical Roman world, the auspex was the state-appointed reader of birds. All public and civic events—war, agriculture, political decisions, and campaigns—were advanced only after this figure's learned interpretation of the calls of birds, or their flights. All birds could be read in terms of these two augural categories. Augury's task was not to foretell the future, but to interpret the will of the gods for the present, by means of readings of given appearances and surfaces in the natural world, so as to guard good relations between gods and the social actions of men. This was the case in Greece, in Etruria, in Rome, and the practice was continued in Roman territories until the fifth or sixth centuries of the current era, when Christ in his tree gradually replaced the older auspices. Fortunatus, Bishop of Poitiers, a sixth-century Merovingian poet, wrote of this tree:

> among all others a unique unchanging tree
> no woodland brought forth such a leaf, flower, shoot;
> sweet tree sustaining a sweet burden with a sweet nail.[4]

In the Easter hymns of Fortunatus, the nightingale sang for a resurrected Christ.

Through the art of augury, the significance of the shapes of flocks and murmurations, number, kind, relation to weather, season, time and industry, and the quality of cry makes the bird a participant in human history. Neither human nor bird can be interpreted in isolation. Reading birds schematized a fundamental relationship between a community and an environment. Not only birds—gemstones, trees, winds, the face of the sky, the internal organs of sheep, the face of water, flowers: the images that moved within poems were not proper to poems; they connected the poems to a lived-in geographical terrain. But here I'm talking about birds. I'm talking about reading the nightingale.

The nightingale is a bird whose image is vocal. It sings both day and night, but the daysong is masked by the abundance of diurnal cacophony. At night, all night long in May, its nesting season, its limpid song animates the landscape in a complex, extended melodic pattern of call and response. The nightingale rarely appears, staying hidden in dense thickets, forests, rural hedgerows, precisely the environments that twentieth-century agricultural and development practices have diminished. Now this song, once common across Europe, is rarely heard. Not only has nightingale habitat almost disappeared, but insecticide use is destroying its food sources. In the non-presence of nightingale song in Europe, we can read the current political economy and ecological crisis. This diminishment of vocal abundance in the social landscape is part of the Capitalocene history of violence. This history is contemporary, but it reaches back.

In the eleventh, twelfth, and thirteenth centuries, nightingale song would have been unexceptional and ubiquitous in May, over the verse territory extending from the Loire River valley southwards to the Mediterranean, and from the southern part of the Atlantic coast inland, eastwards into the Massif Central—comprising present-day Poitou, Limousin, Auvergne, Gascony, and Provence. This territory was not then a part of France, which didn't yet exist as a political state, and it was not French-speaking, but Occitan-speaking. It was one limited kingdom, among several equivalently powerful ones. It named itself after its language—Languedoc (*langue d'Oc*). The region was politically linked to the kingdoms of Aragon, Catalonia, Sicily, and France, and through William IX of Aquitaine's granddaughter Eleanor of Aquitaine (who married Henry II of England and whose sons became English kings) to England. Like all these Christian polities, the Languedoc answered to the office and laws of the Pope in Rome, and briefly Avignon.

The Occitan language was one of several early Romance vernaculars that had differentiated from vulgar Latin, not only in quotidian use, but also in legal charters, contracts, and other secular documents. As well as Latin, it carries traces of Germanic roots in its vocabulary. (Within Occitan, many community dialects flourished, such as Shaudit, understood by other Occitan speakers, but with some Hebrew-derived vocabulary, whose last speaker died in 1977.) Occitan was always a written language—it shows no developmental movement from oral towards written modalities. Its earliest documented appearance was in the refrain of an anonymous polylingual alba, or dawn-celebrating poem, otherwise written in medieval Latin, and found in a tenth-century manuscript:

> Dawn now breaks; sunlight rakes the swollen seas;
> Ah, alas! It is he! See there, the shadows pass![5]

"L'alba part umet mar atra sol / Poy pasa bigil / mira clar tenebras": the Occitan refrain repeats three times, between the Latin stanzas. Some literary historians suggest that the Occitan refrain's presence in the Latin poem links to women's folk songs combined with a tradition of watchman's songs.[6] In Occitan poetry, oral performance was not an iteration of a mythologized preliterate origin, but a complex expression, coexisting with rather than preexisting written composition, transcription, and readerly practice. This widely spoken and written language was not banned from legal and administrative documents until the sixteenth century, one hundred years after the seizure of the Aquitaine by the French crown, at which point the language was consigned to a popular, oral margin by the centralizing French government, which was imposing a monolingual nation-state. The more recent oral status of Occitan is thus the result of an enforced colonial marginalization. But for three centuries Occitan was the international language of lyric poetry, a poetry that upsets the Romantic binary projection of a development of poetry from a primitive oral expression towards the complex literacy associated with modernity and its institutions. Occitan poetry emerged in full, written sophistication, and its international value as the language of poetry was founded in its innovations in style and form—"sweet new style" was how Dante and the *stile nuovo* poets of the Italian vernacular referred to it.

Neither Occitan nor any of the other new Romance vernaculars discussed by Dante in *De Vulgari Eloquentia*—Catalan, Lombard, French, Tuscan—constituted a national language. Each was composed of an unbordered abundance of regional, community, and institutional dialects in complex interrelationships formed by travel, reading, borrowing, citation, manuscript circulation, song, poems, and transcultural institutional settings, such as the Church and its judicial systems, the new universities, political marriages, the dualist Christian heresy called Catharism, and secular legal administrations. The Occitan of troubadour poetry composition and performance was a transgeographical, synthesized language, with traces of Poitvin and Limousin, and a specialized abstract vocabulary that was highly differentiated from that of institutional Latin, and also, in some usages, separate from the spoken Occitan of daily life. In a time when all people were polylingual, the Occitan of poems was just one among several languages current in the region. It's worth insisting here that monolingualism, and the soft concept of "mother tongue," a twelfth-century Church ideological project, are state and ecclesiastical constructions designed to limit, contain, and fix governable subjects.[7] If there is a common state of linguistic experience, it is buoyantly translingual. People move among languages. Occitan's value, both literary and political, was located not in its purity, but in its mobility and its open relationships with other languages, including Latin, Hebrew, and Arabic. Important new terms in the Occitan conceptual vocabulary—words like *rime* and *joi*, were formed on multiple roots by polylingual speakers.[8] Through poetry, Occitan constituted an unbordered vocal community. It was this community that referred to the abundantly differentiated song of birds, and sometimes people's own speech, as their latin.

Here I'm speaking my latin.

The latin sung by the nightingale: what did it sound like? Here is Pliny's description, in his *Natural History*:

> The song of the nightingale is to be heard, without intermission, for fifteen days and nights, continuously, when the foliage is thickening, as it bursts from the bud; a bird which deserves our admiration in no slight degree. First of all, what a powerful voice in so small a body! its note, how long, and how well sustained! And then, too, it is the only bird the notes of which are modulated in accordance with the strict rules of musical science. At one moment, as it sustains its breath, it will prolong its note, and then at another, will vary it with different inflexions; then, again, it will

break into distinct chirrups, or pour forth an endless series of roulades. Then it will warble to itself, while taking breath, or else *disguise* its voice in an instant; while sometimes, again, *it will twitter to itself*, now with a full note, now with a grave, now again sharp, now with a broken note, and now with a prolonged one. Sometimes, again, when it thinks fit, it will break out into quavers, and will run through, in succession, alto, tenor, and bass.[9]

Extremes in tempo, melodic variation, and subtle modulation are key traits of this song, and such technical aspects of sound production command its description. But Pliny additionally ascribes the capacity for disguise to the nightingale, as well as self-address; these reflexive nuances link the bird to conventions of rhetorical stance and volition, and accordingly, to the psychic opacities and social feints of subjectivity—in his text, as in the troubadour songs, a transspecies potency. Pliny further explains that each individual nightingale has its own song, with its own variations, and that this bird is capable of not only learning, from humans, music, and other birds, but also teaching. These capacities, alongside the individual song signature of each bird, are the abilities that link the bird to poets. Nightingales have voices. And what constitutes a "voice" is precisely this complex valence: productive technique, or instrumentality, alongside or simultaneous to the troubled texture of corporeality, or what Roland Barthes referred to as "grain" in his 1972 essay "The Grain of the Voice."[10] Here Barthes critically opens this doubled agency within the field of vocal music. A voice simultaneously communicates, having recourse to technical conventions and physiological training, and it withholds, compellingly animated by an unquantifiable corporality. For Barthes, the grain is this movement-in-stillness that brings the carnality of the incommunicable to inflect the technical apparatus of vocal production. "The grain is the body in the voice as it sings, the hand as it writes, the limb as it performs," he says (188). "The song must speak, must *write*—for what is produced at the level of the geno-song is finally writing" (185). He identifies this geno-song, the subtechnical, carnal aspect of song, as "a space of pleasure, of thrill, a site where language works for *nothing*, that is, in perversion" (187). Within song there is a displacement. There is space for incommunicative resonance, precisely those aspects of experience, those perversions, those heresies, be they erotic or political or both, that must not appear in documents. But there is also in the voice what we could characterize as a third valence, which I'll tentatively call subjectivity, intending this term to refer to the historical movement and address, the enunciation, in Émile Benveniste's terminology, which is always part of linguistic performance. The voice, opening in the corporeality of desire, moves towards unknowable others, others who may be situated in several simultaneous times. There is the sociality of the complex present inherent in the vocal act, there is its inflection with a historical specificity, in terms of both conscious intention and unconscious inflection, whether traumatized or joyous, and there is in it the potential or hope of unthought futures. Subjectivity here will indicate the dynamic transtemporality of social desire. The nightingale is the vocal image of this multivalenced grain.

What we hear in the voice is the temporal movement of knowledge. This knowledge extends in several simultaneous directions, beyond individuated frameworks of selfhood, towards the others who challenge and destabilize any experience of the speaker as autonomous. The surge towards the only fleetingly knowable strangeness of the other and the other's time, *trobar*, is performed by love's voice.

Rime is an epistemological lens.

We don't know whether birds actually spoke in forests, in captivity. We can choose to disbelieve the reports. But we know that birds speak in poems, and it is in poems that we continue to listen to the long duration of voices in their material and subjective interlacing. Birds in troubadour poems are figures of the problematics of voice—they give us an image of how the writers of these poems, a thousand years ago now, imagined what voice was, how it acted and moved in language. Simultaneously formal *and* political, which is to say carnal, the voice shifts and draws its urgency from the flicker of the presence and absence of others. In the lyric poem, the voice of the nightingale is predicated on a silence, and a silencing. Here I am considering that whenever there is a voice, there is always also a suppression of voice, whether through the passive and sometimes self-performed erasure of disbelief and avoidance, or through a symbolic or historical act of force. If the suppressed story of force is threaded back into lyric's history, the poem's voice then performs a political task.

In Ovid's *Metamorphoses*, Philomela, a daughter of the King of Athens, was changed into a nightingale. This is her story. She was raped by Tereus, King of Thrace, her sister's husband, and in livid anger she told him she would now inform the world of his crime—so he cut out her tongue. "The severed tongue lies palpitating on the dark earth, faintly murmuring," moving to its mistress's feet, says Ovid's visceral description.[11] Held captive in a hut in the forest for a year, Philomela made a purple and white weaving, writing into the woven pattern the story of the rape. By means of a messenger, she sent the textile—which was perhaps a shawl or other garment—to her sister Procne, who read on it the purple line of Philomela's absence. Disguised as a bacchante amidst her marauding band of women, Procne then came and rescued her mutilated sister. In horrific revenge, the two sisters killed and cooked the son of Procne and Tereus, to whom they then fed the murdered child, before bringing to him, in fury, the boy's head. The enraged king pursues the sisters, who, flying from him, develop wings—Philomela a nightingale's and Procne a swallow's. Procne flies to the roof, and Philomela escapes to the woods.

What part of Philomela's story lingers in the often insouciantly cited songs of the troubadours? Where is *that* nightingale, violated and transformed? Although Ovid is cited as a possible source for Occitan poets, it is the Ovid of *The Art of Love*, an often bawdy and satirical text teaching the craft of efficient seduction. Not that raucous sexual satire doesn't have a ready stage in troubadour poems, especially in some of the presumed earlier ones of William IX of Aquitaine. But here I want to say that Philomela, with her horrible wound, her severed tongue and replete, textile silence, presents herself not as a narrative content or influence in the troubadour corpus, but as an incipient vocal texture, an impersonal grain, in Barthes's sense, that troubles and figures the subsurface of composed song. There is, inherent to the structure of lyric, an animating vocal redoubling that works beneath or in spite of signification, which here I will name "nightingale."

When the nightingale sings in the troubadours' poems, the poets use the verbs *volf, refrahn, aplana* to describe what they hear: "turns," "echoes," "planes." "Echo" is one possible translation for the verb *refranh*, which has entered both French and English from Occitan as "refrain." (I cite these verbs from the first stanza of the mid-twelfth-century Jaufre Rudel poem beginning with the line "Quan lo ruis de la fontana," which, like the William IX of Aquitaine poem I began with, starts with a time-signature: "When the fountain rivulet / brightens as it comes / so it looks like a flower of eglantine / and the nightingale on the branch turns / and echoes and refines / its sweet song and planes / it's right that I take up my own refrain" (Goldin 102; I have altered his translation to include the English "refrain," paralleling the final word *refranha* in the Occitan). *Refranh* is the descriptive verb associated with nightingale song throughout the troubadour corpus. It has been translated as "modulates" (Goldin),[12] "starts again" (Jacques Roubaud, Fr. *reprends*),[13] and "reiterates" (Paul Blackburn).[14] We now consider a refrain to be a repeating melodic motif that structures a longer composition. Also, the Latin word-root *frain* indicates a breaking, as in fracture, or fragment, or fractal, or reining in: a figurative form of breaking or braking. Refrain: an again-break.

There are not very many troubadour poems that use what we now would consider a refrain, but all of the poems interweave their lines and stanzas, as well as their images and concepts, by means of the structured interlinking of repeating sound values called "rime," and all the poems use a restricted vocabulary, in which certain key words and their derivatives—"joy" and "sweetness" for example—repeat even within the same line, and often from stanza to stanza. These are the first European written texts to have used rime, which we could consider as the smallest refrain-gesture. And in these poems, this break or cut, then re-beginning, is the vocal signature used to indicate the nightingale, both in the conventional verb choice *refrahn*, and in the musical scores for the poems. There are 250 scored poems that still exist, in a body of 2,600 preserved poems; in these, the word *rossignol*, "nightingale," is always musically accompanied by "a breaking in the musical arc," an upwards fluctuation, then a sharp fall, according to an analysis of the musically annotated poems containing the word *nightingale*, by Christelle Chaillou-Amadieu.[15]

The innovation of rime in Occitan written song in the eleventh century was part of a broader transformation of the rhythmic structure of spoken vernacular language. Where spoken Latin was metrically quantitative, prescriptively structuring its oral cadences by means of the fixed long or short vocal duration of vowel sounds, Occitan and the newly forming Romance languages had moved towards a qualitative vocalization, where cadence was patterned on stressed syllables, as spoken English continues to be stressed. Intermediary to this transition was Vulgar Latin, which around the ninth century began to develop a stressed accentuation while retaining some aspects of quantitative meter. To reiterate, a key difference between durational and stressed accents, is that durational stress is fixed and conventional. Each vowel sound has an assigned, stable metrical value. But stressed accent, new in the tenth century, is mobile, contingent, determined by contextual semantics and expressive urgency.

The changing vocal stress patterns were related to innovations in ecclesiastical chant; Saint Martial Abbey, the home of a widely regarded music school, library, and scriptorium, in the Limousin region adjoining the Poitou, was an intense matrix for these new musical and vocal developments. Saint Martial was founded in 848, and by 1065 was famous throughout Europe for music and literature, both sacred and secular. Monks, scholars, poets, and musicians would overwinter there, to make use of the library and enjoy intellectual camaraderie. Some of the earliest troubadour songs, with their musical notations, were preserved in manuscripts at this abbey. The stressed, late-Latin chant metrics originating at Saint Martial influenced, or were perhaps appropriated by, the troubadour vernacular songs of the same region, songs themselves almost exclusively secular. But the writers of the secular vernacular songs took the new stressed rhythms to innovative extremes. Occitan augmented stressed syllables, and had a greater variation of stress patterns, since stress was influenced by meaning. This new presence of variable vocal stress patterns offered a compositional pliability for poems.

In this soundfield, rime—the echo of stressed sounds—appeared. In his songs, William IX of Aquitaine placed the rime at line ends as metrical markers, but just as importantly, internally, within phrases and lines. Rime's work breaks the forward movement of the song by recycling sound values, so that the listener, but also the composer and the singer, is brought to rethink, reopen, the given meanings, and create links, interlacings, between phonemes that work as sonic ornaments at the same time as they complicate and regroup concepts across the time-structure of the song. Rime thus transforms song into a site for the complex rethinking and reactivating of time and emotion. It performs a submerged history, in fragments. The semantic links spun out between words by formal sound echoes give the hearer the space to imagine and inhabit alternative histories and meanings. Rime breaks open the unity of time, as well as the unity of the sign, constructing meaning as a set of relationships in movement, where this movement takes place in the polytemporal consciousness of the reader, the writer, and the performer, who carry the line forward at the same time as they make new associations on the warp of previous phrases and sounds. These associations can be either intentional or unconscious in both their composition and their interpretation. Indeed, rime can open the ear to previously unintuited knowledge and association, within the compositional moment. Part of rime's work occurs in the space of belatedness. This rime entered song through writing, itself a redoubled temporal practice. Any writer spends as much time moving backwards in the text as forward, in a cognitive pleating. The vocal redoubling of the Occitan refrain acted in the distancing, polytemporal capacities of written composition to emerge in the lyric as rime. The attentive space between rimes can frame glimpses of suppressed and silenced meaning: in the time of the return, Philomela, now nightingale, may face us.

Rime, Latin *rhythmus* (m), French *rime* (f), Occitan *rim* (m), as well as *rima* (f): a new word in twelfth-century Occitan, with double origins, as revealed by the dual gendering of the word's variants. The masculine gender is a trace troubling the philological convention of its reception from the Latin, adding a semantic variant.[16] *Rim* is more than rhythm—it is the active field of the making and reception of verse. (The word *poetry* did not become current for verse activity until the sixteenth century.) Paul Zumthor, in his essay "Du rhythme à la rime," says *rime* appeared in Provençal and Old French in the twelfth century, a semantic mutation formed in part on Middle German *Reim*. *Rim* was the word for song, song's making and reception, but also an edgework:

A hoop-shaped piece of wood that forms the outer
   edge of a sieve
surface of water
the outer ring of a wheel

a circular mark or object
a lip
a caul
a pellicule
a leather strap or thong
the perineum
sea-rim

Rime then is an edge-condition, a threshold, that moves vocality and meaning across time-signatures, borders, languages. Barthes's concept of grain can help us understand the polyvalent movements of rime, which is indeed "the very precise space (genre) of *the encounter between a language and a voice*" (181).

It is time to enter more specifically into rime's grain. Consider again the sound values of the opening stanza of the William IX of Aquitaine poem:

Ab la dolchor del temps novel
Foillo li bosc e li auzel
Chanton chascus en lor lati
Segon lo vers del novel chan
Adonc esta ben c'om s'aisi
D'acho don't hom a plus talan[17]

In terms of end rime, the structure of this first stanza, and the second one, is a/a/b/c/b/c—already intricate in terms of the establishment of a tight structure of sonic expectation and its subsequent complication and deferral. (Later stanzas further diversify the sound-structure.) But the *first* words of each line set up a different and concurrent echo-pattern—the opening *a* of *Ab* not repeating till the fifth line's a*donc*, reversed in the sixth line's opening *D'acho*, and the whole series structured around the soft *o's* introduced within the key-word *dolchor*, "sweetness," in the opening line. The digraph consonant in *dolchor* leads to its iteration in *Chanton* ("sings"); *chascus* ("each"); *chan* ("again"); and *d'acho* (that which). The entire stanza is built on "sweetness," *dolchor*, and its inevitable interlacing with "song," "novelty," "leaf," and "man" via the round vowel. Rime's meaningful action is not simply the repetition of sounds, but the construction of strong and supple nonlinear and transtemporal relationships between signifiers. Rime makes voice. Rimes are social facts, and they are structures of memory.

As for *dolchor*—the Latin terms for sweetness, *suavis* and *dulcis* (nearly synonymous), had a specificity not shared by comparable words in Hebrew and Greek. Their connotation was necessarily social: somebody in particular is loved, healed, or persuaded. Sweetness was an attribute that moved between discourses—medicine, cuisine, love, rhetoric, and theology all required sweetness. Sweetness moves fluidly between bodies. We might consider *dolchor* as an aptitude for the reception of desire, in its many social forms.[18] We move towards praise. Rather than a quality, the Latin term designates a culture. Sweetness is communal. This made for problems in translation. Augustine, discussing the translation of the sweetness—Vulgate Latin *suavitas*—of the fruit of knowledge in Genesis, said that sweetness could be evil, or evilness sweet, so in place of *dulcis* or *suavis*, in other instances he proposed goodness, *bonitas* (Carruthers, 94). Goodness is static.

If the stanza is structured on and around the word *dolchor*, through its network of inner rime it also speaks an absent word—*amor* ("love"). This shimmer of withheld, withdrawn, or deferred naming lights the inner textures of troubadour poems. The poets refer within their poems (since often these avant-gardists do write about writing) to the compositional technique of inter-lacement—*entrebascor*—which has a textile reference (one of the proposed origins of these poems is in women's collective weaving and embroidering songs[19]), and also a carnal one, an intertwining technique of kissing. The riming syllables are intertwined as threads, as kisses, as embraces, as garments fallen to the floor.

Paul Zumthor, in his 1973 essay "Les Paragrammes chez les troubadours?," posits that troubadour poets may have used the technique of the paragram, where the scattered syllables of source-words present themselves phonemically below the coded surface of the text. In this compositional theory, a key word is broken into phonemic subunits, then distributed across a line, or even among lines, adding an alternative temporality and substrata of meaning to the explicit voicing and melodic surface of the text.[20] Zumthor's essay is strongly influenced by the then-recent publication of Saussure's work on paragrams in Latin poetry, so evocatively presented by Jean Starobinski in his 1963 essay, and later book, translated in 1979 as *Words upon Words: The Anagrams of Ferdinand de Saussure.*[21] For Zumthor, who proposed that the word *amor* might be the hidden phonemic motor of the five early troubadour poems in his study, this subtextual phonemic seeding of the poem acts to open up the work of signification in language, beyond the closure of the sign, and towards a polysemic complexity (55–67). There is much uncertainty in Zumthor's thesis, as there also was for Saussure, in his ambivalent discovery of the fragmented names of gods and goddesses as scattered substructures of Latin poems. But this ambivalence is itself attractive, a form of scholarly vulnerability and risk that invites a rethinking of fixed assumptions about the work of meaning in language. What if language is not structured on the dual sign, material signifier supporting conceptual signified? Could part of the poem's work, the work performed by rime, be the deferral or even disavowal of the closure of the sign, in favor of a generative, distributed subsong?

For these thinkers, as for the troubadour poets, the poem is the privileged site for a practice of meaning-play and elaboration that surpasses binary teleologies and the institutionally enforced closure of codes. The disengagement from fixed signification, which can be enacted by submerged vocal subsongs or rime, makes a site for the appearance of what's hidden, what's erased culturally, whether this hidden story is the violence of colonialism and misogyny, as in Philomela's song, or the heretical affirmation of shared techniques of joy, of sweetness, of social abundance, as in troubadour lyric. In his analysis of the troubadour poems, while admitting the difficulty of definitively proving the paragram theory, Zumthor proposes that these "letter games," as he calls them, subvert syntagmatic meaning structure "by bursting open [rational] units in a virtual infinity." "The text," he continues, "rocks in the attention and in the memory of the listener, undoing itself in its hypophonic effects, or, extending them, recomposes itself, in an unending game of significatory uncertainty" (66, my translation). I do find it possible to hear the resequenced sounds of the word A-M-O-R flickering beneath the surface of William IX of Aquitaine's line "Ab la dolchor del temps novel." For Zumthor, this cognitive rocking suggests the emergence of a different law of meaning, one that defies the conventions of univocal clarity to establish a metalinguistic torsion as the heart of the song. This torsion is another name for Philomela's escape, an escape that reveals the semantic impoverishment and ultimate violence of binary models of signification.

It's conventional for contemporary readers of the trouba-dour poems to accept the centrality of the concept of "love," *amor*, so it doesn't seem surprising that Zumthor chose *amor* as the keyword for his paragram research. But it's crucial to pause and attempt to let go of the current sentimentalized, sometimes market-driven, and overwhelmingly private understandings of this value. Such misrecognition of *amor* is part of a tradition of the critical appropriation of troubadour poetry into dominant cultural and political ideologies.[22] There exists a cultural politics of medievalism. The term *courtly love*, for example, is not found in the poems, but was an invention of nineteenth-century French medievalists whose allegiances were nationalist, Catholic, and conservative. The Occitan term used in the poems is *fin amor*—something like "ultimate love" or "love abundance." For the poets, singers, philosophers, and theologians of the eleventh, twelfth, and thirteenth centuries, love was a diverse discourse, at once Christian, secular, and mystical.

In her chapters on troubadour verse in *Tales of Love*, Julia Kristeva discusses Bernard of Clairvaux's fourfold structure of affect: Love, Joy, Fear, and Sadness.[23] Clairvaux (1090–1153), who was William IX of Aquitaine's contemporary, spent eighteen years writing sermons on the relation between human and divine love in the Song of Songs. Affect in his thought is located in the soul, following Augustine's theory of affect in *De quantitate animae*, but is dependent on the senses, as well as the will. How do the bodily senses come to take part in the love of God, or in God's love of us? Affect was basically passive in his philosophy—it needed an outside agent to set the soul in motion. Affect was set in movement by the desire for another. Only by means of this sensual movement can we enter God's love. For Clairvaux, human love is an expression and revelation of divine love, but must include sensual expression and experience. Beauty and pleasure are parts of God's love within us. This all-permeating twelfth-century discourse of love was also secular, deriving some of its carnal delight, play, and social problematics from Ovid, whose adage, "Love must be ruled by art," functions as one key to the troubadour experiment. (*The Art of Love* had been translated to Old French in the eleventh century by Chretien de Troyes.) And for the mystical thinkers of Catharism, whose geographical and cultural region overlapped with the troubadours', the expression of love was structured by a thorough dualism, separating body from spirit through individual and community ascetic practices. An additional thread in love's discourse was the Platonic theory of love in the *Symposium* and *Timeaus*, translated in fragments by the early medieval Arab philosophers, who brought their discussions and transcriptions to the Andalusian universities, during the period of the *Convivencia*, between 800 and 1150. Connected to this rich tri-cultural moment in southern European history were the Sufi and Kabbalist mystic writings on love. In the troubadour poems, *amor* was at the core of a secular cosmology connecting human erotic love and its deferral and sublimation to ecstatic experiences of temporality and nature. (Jacques Lacan, in a 1960 seminar on troubadour *fin'amor*, referred to this sublimating practice in troubadour culture as an "ethics of erotics."[24])

Amor, an ideal at once social, ethical, and moral, was thus a set of expressive conventions and sublimating erotic experiments with links to mystical experience. These experiments structured the collective, community expression of joy through song, its parallel convention. Joy and song sought new form. In Jacques Roubaud's thinking on the troubadours, "song" and "love" are the same: "Song, which is, as I have called it, the unifying sign, the sign in movement from love to poetry."[25] Song and love are chosen acts, submitted to generative constraints. They are transmitted cultural shapes. And they are not solely human—the nightingale loves: love *is* its song. "The little wild nightingale / I heard its joy / in love, through its language / and he makes me die of envy," wrote Gaucelm Faidit. "In the leaves he gives love. . ." (Roubaud 272, my translation). The nightingale is the model for human love, which is also sung in rime. For both poet and bird, "language," *lati*, is love's instrument, the mode of identity of song and *amor* in the milieu of a shared social world not separate from nature. And the spaces of love were enclosed—garden, bedchamber, stanza. This bird/song/love identity is one of a group of core images at work in troubadour poems. Bernart Ventadour sang, "The nightingale beneath the leaves / sings from love."[26] In Simone Weil's estimation of Occitan culture, as she explores in her essay "L'Inspiration Occitane," love is the opposite of force.[27] It is a good proportion that bears repeating: Love is the opposite of force. Also, then, song is the opposite of force. That this love, *amor*, was a secular experiment, and that an entire culture, the Languedoc, was organized to welcome, share, and prolong it within the gentle constraints of new experiments in erotic social play and song, made it a scandal from the point of view of the Church. William IX of Aquitaine was two times excommunicated by Pope Innocent II.

The generative movement between secular moral categories and cultural expressions constitutes the core wager of the Occitan song culture. Here I want to stress that the concept or category of the moral was not a punitive limitation, but an opening towards a flourishing human abundance not separate from nature. This abundance deepened and diversified relationship rather than possession. Within the poems, any given ideal can only be approached with the aid of a cluster of influencing and overlapping interdependent moral values. Of all of these—which as well as "love" and "song," include *pretz* ("worth" or "merit"), *dolchor* ("sweetness"), *auzel* ("bird"), *midon* ("lady"), *parage* ("non-hierarchical obedience" [again in Simone Weil's definition])—the most animate ideal, the energy of all value in the world, the word present in almost every poem, is "joy," *joi*. Where "love" is one of the human soul's affections, "joy" has a more ambient, mystical connotation. It moves across and among other concepts, harmonizing. Joy not only radiates through love to express the essence of the poetry; it is the collective ideal of the culture, the most esteemed and essential quality, without which no other value could appear. In the poems *joi* pertains to a general radiant ecstasy that eclipses and yet permits personal emotion. Joy's mystical enthusiasm animates all aspects of life, human and natural. In Bernart de Ventadorn's lark poem, we "see the lark moving / its wings in joy against the light / rising up into forgetfulness, letting go, and falling / for the sweetness that comes to its heart."[28] Joy in the poems is anterior to love, but not separate from it. If love is the opposite of force, then joy is the opposite of death, which is defined as joy's absence.[29] The purpose of Occitan society was to serve joy, as a lover serves their beloved—through the evasion and reversal of any act or intention of force. Song served life.

The Occitan word *joi*, which was masculine in gender, derived from the Latin *gaudium* (neut.). It appeared for the first time in a poem of William IX of Aquitaine. A key scholar of William, Alfred Jeanroy, theorizes that *joi* was a Poitvin, or Poitou-area, addition to Occitan.[30] In Occitan, the derivatives from Latin *gaudium* retain the hard *g* and the *a* sound—*gai*, for example, is an Occitan word formed on *gaudium*. But the soft *j* and the movement from *au* to *oi*, come from the Poitou, William's territory. There are a couple of points to be made about this sonic difference. One is that the first troubadour was not really *from* the Occitan region, he was from the Poitou, which was on the northernmost border of Aquitaine: he inflected his Occitan vocabulary with outside sounds. There is no question here of linguistic purity or propriety. William's Occitan was synthesized. Another of Jeanroy's points is that *joi* was possibly coined *for* use in the written poems—that it may not have come from typically spoken dialects of Poitvin. By extension, Jeanroy hypothesizes that the Occitan of troubadour poems was not a specific regional dialect, but was a *coine*—a synthesized literary language that borrowed traits from several dialects in order to compose a lexicon that was as aesthetically malleable, and as universal in its scope, as possible. Which is to say that the Occitan of the poems was a composed literary language, both inventing and borrowing vocabulary from a range of sources (as noted earlier), not a spoken dialect reflecting a specific region and popular origin.

We don't know for certain if this was the case. But the idea of the Occitan of song as a synthetic language generated by the broad social desire of poets to serve love's joy by means of the composition and exchange of poems is one that I simply want to state here, so it's in the air, as the lark and the nightingale are in the air. The *coine* theory takes poetry away from the univocity of origin narratives and replaces philological romanticization with a distributed commitment to composition as collective happiness. As noted above, the new *joi* of the troubadour poems is a masculine noun in Occitan, differentiating it from the French feminine *joie*. Its meaning and tone are inflected with a robust active vitality, the fluttering of the lark against light. Whereas Latin *gaudium* pertained to sensual experience, *joi* had a wider, ambient mystical, vitalistic jubilance and was very often augmented and interlaced with a clustered series of *j*-sound words meaning "play," "jewels," "days," "enjoyment," "jouissance"—a modulated soundscape where "joy" was its own rime or refrain:

> When the new grass and the leaves come forth
> And the flower burgeons on the branch
> And the nightingale lifts its high
> Pure voice and begins its song
> I have joy in it, and joy in the flower
> And joy in myself, and in my lady most of all;
> On every side I am enclosed and girded with joy
> And a joy that overwhelms all other joys.[31]

This joy, the culture of joy and joy's communal elaboration, was to be colonized and exterminated. In 1209, Pope Innocent III, by means of the French crown, carried out a crusade in this territory of song. Essentially the crusade was a colonizing war, launched in order to destroy all traces of the Christian heresy called Catharism, which included the varied culture that supported and surrounded the heresy.

One branch of a long and diverse tradition of dualism in Christianity going back to the second century, Catharism was by the early medieval times very present in Flanders, Germany, Lombardy, and Gaul, as well as in the Languedoc region. The Cathars and other early dualists believed the institution of the Church was the expression of the Antichrist. They rejected all church authority, and by extension all state power and its institutions, including wealth and its accumulation, marriage and childbearing, and reproductive sexual practices. The Cathars were divided into two groups, the believers and the *parfaits*, these second, after an initiation ritual, taking the sect's acetic practices to an extreme not followed by believers, who could carry out fairly typical household lives, while hosting parfaits in their homes, for meetings and blessings. Usually parfaits were of the aristocratic class, where believers were artisans and peasants, very often weavers, so that the extensive weaving industry in the southwest became associated with the heresy. The Cathar parfaits, women and men, were vegetarian, wore simple black garments, and practiced poverty and itinerant preaching. In the twelfth century, the Catharism of the Languedoc became especially targeted by the Church and the French crown, for complex reasons. The region has very geographically isolated pockets because of its mountainous terrain, and had in its isolation maintained legal and social practices that were different from those of the north. Through the Carolingian Era, women could inherit land, for example, and exercise political power over that land, as well as over monasteries, which were very often co-sex and headed by women. Women also were accepted as *parfaiti*, and in the old nobility of the region, many women were *parfaiti*, or their supporters. Noblemen's and women's homes followed old traditions of hospitality, sheltering free discussion, and mixed social gatherings. Often these same Cathar women were patrons of troubadour poets.

The Languedoc was also a region with a long tradition of coexistence of Christian, Muslim, and Jewish communities. Catharism can be considered as the Christian mystical parallel to Sufism and Kabbalism,[32] whose mystical texts, poets, and students formed a covert network from the Iberian peninsula across the south of the European continent.[33] In the 1180s, when the Church's third crusade against the Muslims in Jerusalem had failed, the kings of England and France returned to the continent with already-formed armies and an explicit directive to defend Church power on their own terrain. During this same period, drought conditions and flooding ruined agricultural yields, leading to widespread famine and illness. Moneylending and borrowing became an important economic survival tactic. There was a tradition of interest in the southwest that countered the Church's moneylending practices— the Church wished only the monasteries to have the power to lend money, interest-free, in order to continue to consolidate social power within the centralized Church structure. Usury was deemed a form of heresy, since interest as an economic custom was explicitly secular. In 1190, Pope Nicholas IV visited the Toulouse area, held a meeting among the Christian nobility, who came from as far as Tours to participate, and a decision was made to militarily appropriate the region. Along with Catharism, targets were usury, fornication (this category included the participation of women in public and religious life, and the wearing of luxurious garments), and the peaceful mixture of peoples—*brassage*, as Simone Weil called it—that had been so instrumental in the emergence of the song culture. This war was launched first of all against the powerful regional dukes of Toulouse, Beziers, and Foix, who refused to follow the French in renouncing Catharism in favor of a consolidated Church. In July 1209, when the crusade began, carried out by Simon de Montfort, an agent of the French king, 20,000 people were slaughtered in two days in the city of Beziers. The French army had applied to the city to surrender their heretics and their Jews; when the city refused, all the citizens were killed. After the fall of Beziers, Montfort's army moved across the region, taking town after town, chateau after chateau, in an almost unchallenged swathe.[34]

It is not known exactly how the culture of the troubadour poets coincided with that of the Cathars, since communication remained necessarily covert, and documents were destroyed in the wake of the war and the ensuing Inquisition. But the two shared a region and a social milieu, and some Occitan historians—Robert Lafont and René Nelli—link the erotic and social experiments of the poetry, as well as its network of patrons, to the anarchical spiritual community, noting that the two groups shared the same patrons, tables, and communities.[35] After 1209, both the poets and the surviving Cathars went underground, went silent, or left—to Italy, to Spain, some to the northern courts of Marie de Champagne (daughter of William IX of Aquitaine's granddaughter Eleanor, Queen of England and Aquitaine), where troubadour formal innovation entered the French language as *trouvère* poetry. The chateaux and their lands were taken over by the army of French crusaders, as war spoils. By 1215, the crusade was completed, and the French agent Montfort was declared the new ruler of Beziers, Toulouse, and Carcassonne. In 1234, the Inquisition was established in Aquitaine to continue to flush out remaining heresy in an ideological extension of the military occupation, through forced confessions and conversions, secret denouncements, torture, burnings, and imprisonments. The outcome of the crusade and the Inquisition was the destruction of the social and political matrix that engendered the troubadour song-culture. In his introduction to his translations of troubadour poems, Jacques Roubaud pointedly says that song was born, and was killed ("Le chant est né et a été tué").[36] There can be no joy in colonized territory.

I think it is time to newly visit the Occitan song project, now because we have so often repeated the atrocity which then cut short that ornate ethics of erotics. We have been the slaughterers. We have foreclosed languages. We have criminalized practices of love that we don't understand. Having echoed the forlorn cut, can we now turn to read the purple writing sent forward to us by Philomela, and find in her deferred voice a space outside force? In the sonorous artifacts we now call poems, there is detailed information about survival, resistance, and just access to communal pleasure.

What was taken by the crusade, and what is continually taken by all subsequent colonizations? Joy is taken, and with it, life. We might ask what happened to the voice, to rime. We still have lyric poetry, which in its aesthetic, rather than social

form, has continued to find institutions to shelter it. We have a
convention of the voice of a poem as being personal, interior to
an individual's experience and sense of being. Now turn. Now
listen again for the nightingale, listen for the subsong. Attend to
Philomela's wound. Can there be a resuturing of rime? I want to
consider the possibility of obedience to a subsong as a collective
ethical practice of joyous abundance.

> Call voice the collective site of the production of rime.
> Call rime an ethics of song.
> The constraints structuring the innovation of rime
>   parallel the constraints expanding love. They are
>   polyphonic.
> Rime dissolves the closure of signification, and the
>   unity of origins, which are ideologically linked.
> All time is simultaneous in rime.
> Love abandons the sign.
> Its destination can't be fully determined, since both
>   history and futurity are parts of its composition.
> Rime dismantles borders by ignoring borders. It migrates.
> Rime marks the essential incompletion of the voice,
>   its necessary turn to love.
> The incompletion accompanies joy.
> This is where Philomela writes herself.

Notes

1. William IX of Aquitaine, "Ab la dolchor del temps novel," in
Lyrics of the Troubadours and Trouvères, ed. and trans. Frederick Goldin
(New York: Anchor Books, 1973), 46–48.

2. Paul Zumthor's essay "Du rhythme à la rime," in *Langue, texte,
énigme* (Paris: Éditions de Seuil, 1975), 125–43, traces the emergence of
this new concept in twelfth-century Occitan *rima* (f) and old French
rime (m) and is discussed below. The theory of the origin of rime as

a technique in troubadour verse varies widely among critics. For the possible relation of rime to medieval Arab women's song in Spain, see Maria Rosa Menocal, *Shards of Love: Exile and the Origins of The Lyric* (Durham, NC: Duke University Press, 1993).

3. William IX of Aquitaine, "Farai un vers de dreyt nien," *Lyrics of the Troubadours and Trouvères*, 25.

4. Fortunatus, *Pange Lingua*; quoted in Mary Carruthers, *The Experience of Beauty in the Middle Ages* (Oxford: Oxford University Press, 2013), 106.

5. A. S. Kline in translation of Anonymous, "With Pale Phoebus" (Brindon Press), October 8, 2019, http://www.brindinpress.com/poanophe.htm.

6. See *Eos: An Enquiry into the Theme of Lovers' Meetings and Partings at Dawn in Poetry*, ed. Arthur T. Hatto (Mouton & Co: The Hague, 1965) 280, 354.

7. In *Shadow Work: Vernacular Values Examined* (London: Marion Boyars, 1981), Ivan Illich discusses the politics of monolingualism.

8. See Paul Zumthor, "Du rhythme à la rime." in *Langue, texte, énigme*. Alfred Jeanroy, introduction to *Les Chansons de Guillaume IX, duc d'Aquitaine* (Paris: Champion, 1913), iii–xxi. He discusses the concept of synthetic vernaculars, making reference to the mixed Poitvin-Latin etymology of the Occitan word *joi*.

9. Pliny, book 10, chapter 43, *Delphi Complete Works of Pliny the Elder* (1855), trans. Bostock and Riley, http://www.perseus.tufts.edu/hopper/text?doc=Perseus%3Atext%3A1999.02.0137%3Abook%3D10%3Achapter%3D43.

10. Roland Barthes, "The Grain of the Voice," in *Image Music Text*, trans. Stephen Heath (New York: Hill and Wang, 1978), 179–89.

11. Ovid, *Metamorphoses,* ed. G. P. Gould, trans. F. J. Miller (Cambridge, MA: Harvard University Press, 1984), 319–35.

12. Frederick Goldin in his translation, *Lyrics of the Troubadours and Trouvères*, ed. and trans. Frederick Goldin (New York: Anchor Books, 1973), 102.

13. Jacques Roubaud in his translation of Jaufre Rudel, "Quan lo ruis de la fontana," in *Les Troubadours*, ed. and trans. Jacques Roubaud (Paris: Seghers, 1980), 74–75.

14. Paul Blackburn in his translation of Jaufre Rudel, "Quan lo ruis de la fontana," *Proensa: An Anthology of Troubadour Poetry*, ed. George Economou, trans. Paul Blackburn (Berkeley: University of California Press, 1978), 70.

15. Christelle Chaillou-Amadieu, "Philologie et Musicologie: Les variants musicales dans les chants de troubadours," in *Les Noces de Philologie et Musicologie: Textes et musiques du Moyen Âge* (Paris: Classiques Garniers, 2017), 69–95.

16. I mention the grammatical genders of words as a linguistic technique for tracing developmental histories of differentiation in semantics, rather than as meaningful designations in themselves.

17. William IX of Aquitaine, "Ab la dolchor del temps novel," in *Les Chansons de Guillaume IX, duc d'Aquitaine*, ed. Alfred Jeanroy (Paris: Champion, 1913), 24–26. As translated by Frederick Goldin, in *Lyrics of the Troubadours and Trouvères*: "In the sweetness of this new season / the woods leaf out, the birds / sing each one in its latin/after the verses of the new song. / This it is right that each man settle down / with what a man wants most."

18. Mary Carruthers's essay "Taking the Bitter with the Sweet," in *The Experience of Beauty in the Middle Ages* (Oxford: Oxford University Press, 2013), offers a strong cultural history of sweetness across discourses in medieval culture.

19. In *Les Troubadours: Une Histoire Poétique* (Paris: Éditions Perrin, 2013), Michel Zink discusses the theory of origin of troubadour verse in women's weaving songs.

20. Paul Zumthor "Les Paragrammes chez les troubadours?," in *Langue, texte, énigme,* 55–67.

21. Jean Starobinski, *Words upon Words: The Anagrams of Ferdinand de Saussure*, trans. Olivia Emmet (New Haven, CT: Yale University Press, 1979).

22. See R. Howard Bloch, "The Birth of Medieval Studies," in *A New History of French Literature*, ed. Denis Hollier (Cambridge, MA: Harvard University Press, 1989), 6–12.

23. Julia Kristeva, *Tales of Love*, trans. Leon S. Roudiez (New York: Columbia University Press, 1987), 151–69.

24. See Jacques Lacan, *The Seminar of Jacques Lacan, Book 7: The Ethics of Psychoanalysis, 1959–1960*, trans. Dennis Porter (New York: Norton, 1992), 139–60.

25. Jacques Roubaud, *La Fleur Inverse: L'art des troubadours* (Paris: Les Belles Lettres, 1994), 271.

26. Bernart Ventadour, "Bel m'es can eu vei la brolha," cited in Thomas Alan Shippey, "Listening to The Nightingale," *Comparative Literature* 22, no. 1 (Winter, 1970), 46–60.

27. Simone Weil, *L'Inspiration Occitane* (Paris: L'Éclat, 2014).

28. Bernart Ventadour, "Can vei la lauzeta mover," *Lyrics of the Troubadours and Trouvères*, 145.

29. Robert Lafont, "Pour lire les Troubadours," *Cahiers du Sud* 372 (1963), 163–79.

30. Alfred Jeanroy, introduction to *Les Chansons de Guillaume IX, duc d'Aquitaine*, xii.

31. Bernart Ventadour, "Can l'erba fresch' e.lh folha par," *Lyrics of the Troubadours and Trouvères*, 136–39.

32. For discussion of the relationship of Kabbalism to Catharism in twelfth-century Provence, see Gershom Scholem, *Origins of the Kabbalah*, trans. Allan Arkush (Princeton, NJ: Princeton University Press, 1990).

33. Henry Corbin discusses the coincidence of troubadour poetry with Catharism and Sufism in his essay "Manichéism et la religion de la beauté," *Cahiers du Sud* 371 (1963). See also Corbin's *Creative Imagination in the Sufism of Ibn Arabi*, trans. Ralph Manheim (Princeton, NJ: Princeton University Press, 1969), 136–44.

34. I have synthesized this account of the Albigensian Crusade and the Cathar heresy from the essays collected in Robert Lafont, Jean Duvenroy, Michel Roquebert, Paul Labal, and Philippe Martel, *Les Cathares en Occitanie* (Fayard: Paris, 1982).

35. René Nelli, *L'Érotique des troubadours* (Toulouse: Privat, 1963).

36. Jacques Roubaud, *Les Troubadours: Anthologie bilingue* (Paris: Seghers, 1971), 2.

Chapter 5

Making-with Nightingales and Ants

A Response to Lisa Robertson

SHANNON MAGUIRE

Lisa Robertson played a sound composition of nightingales, recorded by her partner at their home in the South of France, at the top of her Robert Creeley Lecture, "*Dous Chantar*: Refrain for a Nightingale." Afterwards, she remarked that a "shiver of amazement" runs through her when she listens to these bird voices because they are the same nightingales (many generations down) that inspired the heart-mind sojourns of the twelfth- and thirteenth-century troubadour poets. This frisson between contemporary French experimental sound poetry and the troubadours (writing and singing in the Occitan language) that Robertson opens through her own work seeds a much needed deterritorialization (to borrow a term from Gilles Deleuze and Félix Guattari) of contemporary poetics. Deterritorialization is the process of the ecstatic abandonment of self as a location upon a sociopolitical map, while retaining a situated embodiment. Deterritorialization endangers the organism while also enacting a radical openness to what is beyond the self. This process is not unlike that of a bursting seed, or the germination of the mind when it surges with new thoughts instigated by a bookish encounter.

The tension of forces of increase and obliteration leads Robertson to take careful measure of her poetic materials and the forces that she releases into the world through the micro- and macrostructure of her poetry and poetics. Her work on troubadours is attuned to the dynamics of birdsong and to the interspecies poetics that, rather than leaving permanent marks on a territory, instead created a dynamic wake of exuberant resistance that resonates to this day and resists appropriation even as it invites improvisation. Lucretius personifies Nature as "Faire Venus mother of Æneas race" and maintains that "all things are brought to light by thee / By whom alone their natures goverened be, / From whom both lovelinesse and pleasure springs" in *De rerum natura*.[1] The birds have an important role in Lucretius's invocation to Venus, with which he opens his otherwise materialist poem, a gesture that "translators and commentators have sought to explain . . . since the first critical exegesis on the poem," as Robertson attests.[2]

> Thy power possessing first birds of the ayre
> They thy approach with amorous noates declare,
> Next when desires the savage herd incite
> They swim through streams, and their fat pastures
>   slight
> To follow thee, who in seas, rivers, hills
> In the birds leavie bowers and in greene fields
> Instilling wanton love into each mind,
> Mak'st cereatures strive to propogate their kind.[3]

Perhaps it is the birds here that link Robertson's *3 Summers* (Robertson's most recently published full length collection at the time of the lecture, and one that can be read as an engaged reply to Lucretius) and her work on the troubadours' nightingales. In any case, Robertson's recent poetics put the imperative to increase in tension with the destruction of natural environments that otherwise generation after generation would occupy, as in the case of nightingales that Robertson listens to. For Robertson, "Duration isn't singular / and only beneath its tree a politics / [slow pan of wrecking balls dominates the soundtrack]."[4] Robertson is conversant with Leibniz's nomadology as articulated by Deleuze, and she animates these relations in the service of observing an improvisational subsong that transverses Lucretius, the troubadours, nightingales, and contemporary antitotalitarian poetics and articulates an interspecies, polylingual politics of consciousness. In the multiple, disquiet temporalities evoked by her investigations into the lyric mode, the folds of wings echo in the search for tunes and atonal compositions that can project the differentials of consciousness.

The word *troubadour* is a sixteenth-century French noun indexing a group of lyric poets straddling three countries (southern France, eastern Spain, and northern Italy) during the twelfth-to-fourteenth centuries. It comes from the Occitan verb *trobar,* meaning "to find" and "to invent a song, compose in verse." Its speculative proto-Indo-European root is *TREP-* "to turn," making it a cousin of such words as *contrive, heliotrope, isotropic, psychotropic, retrieve, trope,* and *entropy*—which we now often interpret as the second law of thermodynamics, or noise.[5] However, linguists also propose an alternative derivation from Occitan "from a metathesis of Latin *turbare* 'to disturb,' via a sense of 'to turn up.' Meanwhile, Arabists posit an origin in Arabic *taraba* 'to sing.'"[6] The amplification of disturbance, whether erotic or political, seems an apt description of the way that this secular tradition of song productively transformed the practices and concepts of love and affiliation. Troubadours and trouble are linked through their etymological affinity with the Latin verb *turbare* "to disturb," interlacing song and poetry in a noisy and clamorous history of unsettling orthodoxies by "turning up" the amplitude of disturbance *and* (secular) desire (as heat). Troubadours create the lyric turbulence necessary to swerve orthodoxies from their seats of assumed power. Of course, in queer theory, the action of queering is to trouble and disturb orthodoxies by turning up (as in both uncovering and turning up the volume on) and activating other possibilities, relations, materialities. All of these meanings swell with the fruit in *3 Summers* as in "*Dous Chantar*: Refrain for a Nightingale."

Phyllis Webb argues that "the proper response to a poem is another poem."[7] Elizabeth Grosz reminds us that for Henri Bergson "adapting is not repeating but replying."[8] In this essay, I consider how *3 Summers* can be thought of as a book-length series of long poems that respond and reply to Lucretius's *De rerum natura*, and furthermore, how Robertson's Creeley lecture and work on the medieval troubadours is a discrete yet contiguous response to (and innovative refraining from) the Neoplatonism laced like lead through the neoliberal discourses that saturate the dominant global present.[9] In what follows, I will respond to Robertson's generously turbulent, generative lecture, as well as *3 Summers*, and I will speak to how I see our poetics in conversation (at the request of the poet). Here, then, I offer a baroque poetics for a baroque poetics.

Avant-la-lettre, Avant-l'esprit, and the Specter of Lucretius

Robertson highlights the importance of unlikely and even untimely waves of continuity through a transmission history laden with empirical power and stacked heavily against pleasure when she mischievously curates an encounter between Lucretius and menopause in *3 Summers*. I listened for resonances between two secular materialist verse contexts that never overlapped or knew of each other's existence—Lucretius's atomism and the Occitan writing and singing troubadours—in her Creeley lecture. For as Robertson puts it: "I always thought heresies involved love and discontinuity but now I see that continuity is the revolution" (*3 Summers*, 68).

Institutions of knowledge associated with empire are sites of discontinuity where only those branches of thought that produce fruit for the empire are left to flourish. The University at Toulouse was built by papal bull to extinguish the "heresy" that Robertson discusses with such loveliness in her lecture; the neoliberal university continues this tradition of cherry-picking lineages of thought. Centuries before the University at Toulouse, this Church-led practice of enforced discontinuity affected the possibility of a textual encounter between Lucretius and the troubadours. As Ryan J. Johnson points out:

> The eventual fall of the Roman Empire and the rise of the Christian church inaugurated an almost global campaign to eradicate ancient atomism by seeking to destroy every copy of *De rerum natura*, which had quite a lasting effect, for scholars assumed for almost a thousand years that it was irretrievably lost. It was only in 1417, when the great Italian book hunter Poggio Bracciolini fortuitously encountered it in a German monastery, that atomism returned with full force and spread like a virus throughout early modern Europe . . . [T]hat atomic text carried forth the power of that formative swerve emerging out of the encounter with the theory of atoms that would, much later in the twentieth century, lead to another important event: the French philosopher Gilles Deleuze read *De rerum natura*.[10]

The twelfth- and thirteenth-century troubadours could not have had a direct encounter with Lucretius, but only the traces that they gleaned from Ovid, Virgil, and Cicero—all of whom had been influenced in one way or another by him. Johnson proposes a "minor tradition: of materialist thought: 'atomism, Stoicism, Duns Scotus, Spinoza, Hume, Nietzsche, Bergson, Deleuze, and perhaps now us'" (8), to whom I would add Alfred Whitehead, Hannah Arendt, Isabelle Stengers, Donna Haraway, Elizabeth Grosz, Myra J. Hyrd, Karen Barad, Dorothea Olkowski, and Lisa Robertson, among many others. Likewise, in his introduction to Deleuze's *The Fold: Leibniz and the Baroque*, Tom Conley argues that Deleuze "implies [that Leibniz] develops a philosophy that bridges the pre-Socratics, Lucretius, and neo-Einsteinian thinkers" (xiii). Lucretius's poetry, then, has been a long disquieting prickle in Western knowings and category formation processes.

As I sat listening to Lisa Robertson's rich voice deliver her lecture on a sumptuous early-spring evening in Buffalo in 2018, I felt a strong context and community for the *avant-l'esprit*, *avant-la-lettre* poetics that I, too, engage in: poetics committed to "welcoming and making space for that which cannot yet be imagined or lived," as Elizabeth Grosz puts it.[11] That is, poetry that summons new forms and arrangements of letters and sounds, and moves beyond language *as such* to incorporate the sonic fabric of existence and hold space for communications among nonhuman actors. Donna Haraway's *Staying with the Trouble: Making Kin in the Chthulucene* is an uncanny companion text for Robertson's recent texts.[12] These texts operate within a field of thought that instantiates what Haraway calls: "sympoiesis: making-with" (5). They share a spirit of breaking open the calcified power of authorship practices while foraging for new connections and relations.

The poem "A Coat" from *3 Summers*, the very title of which is suggestive of Lucretius (about which more below), is dedicated to Robertson's friend Stacy Doris (*3 Summers*, 74), the same Stacy from "Third Summer," with whom she ate artichokes while "discovering the etymology of hormone as star-snot" (98). As Sina Queyras notes: "The poet Stacy Doris, with whom Robertson was collaborating on the 'Perfume Recordist' before Doris died, is very present here."[13] Indeed, Robertson's meditation on this erotic friendship appears as small pleats throughout *3 Summers*. But Robertson's work on noise and its relation to the "return to the sex of . . . thinking" (*3 Summers*, 10) as subsong has many bonds with Doris that extend beyond the limits of *3 Summers* and connects the two of them through reading-writing practice to a materialist lineage that reaches back to Lucretius and in turn links their work more broadly to an *avant-la-lettre* contemporary transnational poetics. *Nilling,* a book of Robertson's prose essays, published in 2012, opens with an epigraph from Stacy Doris's *Knot*: "Form means we keep changing our minds, at every velocity, due to life; poetry is that fact's lucidity,"[14] and it ends with Robertson's dedication: "As I complete my corrections for this book, I mourn the death of my friend and collaborator Stacy Doris, at the age of 49. This *Nilling*, then, marks a profoundly sad closure, and I offer these essays as a modest wreath to Stacy's extraordinary gifts of friendship and poetry."[15] *Nilling* is a book that follows the clinamen of Robertson's readings of Lucretius, Deleuze, Arendt, and Pauline Réage, among others, as she meditates on the limits and porosities of will, duration, and im/materiality.

Yes, a specter is haunting *avant-l'esprit, avant-la-lettre* sympoiesis—the specter of Lucretius. Lucretius was a Roman poet-physicist whom Robertson has long been dialoguing with:

> I began to read Lucretius in Cambridge in 1999, while researching the sources for Virgil's *Georgics*. At first, I read the Penguin Classics edition. When that became too tattered to carry with me any longer, I switched to the French prose translation from Les Belles Lettres, bought in the 6th arrondissement fairly expensively in 2002. In early 2006 I went to read Lucretius in London. I don't know why I came to read [Pauline Réage's *Histoire d'O*, Hannah Arendt's *The Life of the Mind*, and Lucretius' *De rerum natura*] in tandem, but

the accident of doing so . . . may say something about
how reading constitutes itself as a deeply contingent
topos, fraught by various agencies . . . Among these
agencies figures the troubling potential of negation,
even abnegation, as a cognitive force.[16]

The accident of reading these three texts in detail together lead
her to the following observation:

An Epicurean moment circulates among the three texts.
Arendt cites the "*lathe biosas*," live in hiding, one of
the tenets of the Epicurean School of Athens. Lucretius'
poem is a study in Epicurean physics and ethics, as
well as a complex form of praise for his chosen master.
In certain views, Réage may represent a popularized
interpretation of Epicureanism as a commitment to
sensual and erotic excess. I think this shared Epicurean
moment is accidental, a kind of fall, as Derrida calls
it in "My Chances," his essay on Lucretius, Freud and
the *clinamen*. ("Lastingness," 25)

I agree with Robertson, while emphasizing the "live in hiding"
aspect of a suppressed epistemology frayed into 100,000 threads
(or sentences) scattered over time and space. In considering
together Robertson's prose essays and poetry, Donna Haraway's
essays, and my own collection of poetry *Myrmurs: An Exploded
Sestina*,[17] I am tracing a Lucretian current—a voltage, a touch—
that runs through the texts.

In very basic terms, Lucretius believes that the universe was
composed of atoms and void, that the swerve of atoms and the
reactions that their collisions caused explained material existence.
In turn, he views religion as an agent of fear and control (influencing Marx and Engels) and insists that by understanding that
the universe is composed of atoms and their interactions, people
could free themselves:

Why doubt that reason alone can quench this terror
   with its spark,
Especially since life is one long labour in the dark?
And just as children shudder at everything in black
   of night,
So sometimes things we are afraid of in the broad
   daylight
Are only bugbears as tots dread in a darkened room,
And therefore we must scatter this terror of the
   mind, this gloom
Not by the illumination of the sun and bright rays,
But by observing Nature's laws and looking on her face.
(*On the Nature of Things*, book II, l.52–61, pp. 37–38)

Fear and pleasure are both highly agitated, vibratory emotions. For Lucretius, pleasure is the highest common good with emphasis on more long-term kinds of pleasure (such as the pleasure of reading). Lucretius believed that the gods lived in the void between worlds and had no interest in human activities—the best that humans could do was to bear huge, unrequited crushes on the gods, yet this would not add to human pleasure. Instead, Lucretius argued that knowledge of the natural sciences was the basis for free will and liberation from fear of death.

Robertson slyly problematizes Lucretius's convictions in *3 Summers* when she draws a parallel between atoms as the animators of the universe and those most contested twenty-first century elements of biology—hormones:

Stacy and I eating artichokes in the kitchen late
   afternoon
discovering the etymology of hormone as star-snot

I fall asleep I lie awake there is a storm a war an
   illness an agony
how much freedom can be made mentally?

I arrive at the end of nine centuries of rhyme
The theatre of value is having its objects slashed (98)

The idea of cosmic bodies being phlegmy, oozing, sneezing, dripping entities that spread life in a viral or bacterial way is gorgeously heretical to Lucretius's grand unifying theory of atoms that underwrote his project of free will and human happiness. But for Robertson, the question of freedom is complicated by gender and social meanings attached to concepts such as nature, hormone, and sex. Lucretius believed that a fuller understanding of natural processes would lead humanity towards a freedom from the fear of death and by extension—as the manipulation of the fear of death is the mode of sovereign power—freedom from the tyranny of religion and kings. But Robertson's skepticism is more attuned at this point to de Sade than Lucretius insofar as she probes "how much freedom can be made mentally." Robertson's poetic inquiry into freedom is coded in the feminine and, as Angela Carter puts it, de Sade

> describes sexual relations in the context of an unfree society as the expression of pure tyranny, usually by men upon women, sometimes by men upon men, sometimes by women upon men and other women; the one constant to all Sade's monstrous orgies is that the whip hand is always the hand with the real political power and the victim is a person who has little or no power at all, or has it stripped from him. In this schema, male means tyrannous and female means martyrized, no matter what the official genders of the male and female beings are.[18]

This tension that Robertson navigates between her own erotic and poetic materiality and her reading of de Sade is subtly staged in her "slashing" of "objects in the theatre of value," where Robertson rents space for a subsong that begins as noise and renders "any image not lived as commodious / where image is a nilling," an unwanted by-product of patriarchy (in other words, trash) and "would include the total refusal of each existing narrative of / femininity" (*3 Summers*, 39). Robertson, then, searches for what is hidden in the traffic sounds of daily commerce and splashy displays of violence on power's highway, and lifts the subsong as the noise of noise. Here she breaks with de Sade, whom Carter unmasks as being "still in complicity with the authority which he hates" (136) and at final count "a great puritan" who "will disinfect of sensuality anything he can lay his hands on; therefore he writes about sexual relations in terms of butchery and meat" (138). Robertson's subsong, on the contrary, hankers after "vitalist vocal co-movement" and obeys "an incandescent and erotic duration."[19] In a passage from "Disquiet," Roberson explains that last phrase: "Here I use the word 'erotic' as a way of touching upon the expectant unknowability of an apparently passive poetics of reception. There is a psychic and physiological pleasure in the choice of a bodily immersion in the materiality of this uncontrollable outside that accompanies the time of a tensile listening. One becomes a subject in the barest sense: a contingent point of coordinated perception of and response to temporal specificity" ("Disquiet," 61). In this way, Roberson instantiates an *avant-la-lettre, avant l'esprit* poetics that extends outwards and away from certain avant-garde poetics that, like de Sade's writings, are complicit with authority, no matter how much they doth protest to the contrary, and are of the puritanical bent of fleshless, senseless butchery and meat, autopsy reports and judiciary statements of facts. Robertson is ultimately after what she calls the "ambient vernacular."[20]

In "An Awning," difference, repetition, idea, and thought expose an erotics that explicitly meditates on Lucretius's "The Senses." This passage from early in Lucretius's book IV, "The Senses," is one to which Robertson returns over and over in *3 Summers*:

Now there's another matter
Of vital importance that I must explain. Let me begin
By saying there are images of things—a sort of skin
Shed from the surfaces of objects, from the outer layer—
Films that drift about this way and that upon the air.
And it is rather *images* of things, these films, that make
Our minds afraid when we encounter them while
we're awake.[21]

Consider Robertson's two stanzas on page 109 of *3 Summers* that begin with the lines, "Always something flows fatally from each surface / streaming outwards with smoothness for a rapid origin / with thinness in many ways all at once" as if invoking pixels or social media displays from FetLife or PornHub, "now again streaming they brush our pupils and pass into us like air / like colour like fingers little by little they give us the image of our / bodies/ as ideas bobbing and melting and incessantly chang-ing shape." As if the Neoplatonism of hypermobile, proprietary media that serve the ideals of heteropatriarchal capitalism exist in the same black box in which Lucretius places his untouchable, untouching gods. Yet, there is also something both enslaving and tantalizing about their very mobility and motility. Robertson asks: "Is all epistemology metaphorical?" and replies to herself: "Quite free of assignment / and despite the inclement representations/ the theatre of an idea / is having its breast stroked / —just enough to subvert the conditions of transmission—not wanting to reproduce a friendship but to repeat it" (109). Here she's troubled and queered the constitutive assumptions that precede Western categories of gender and sex to such an extent that when she returns to the software known as hormones, it's so out of sync with masculinist assumptions about the binary "drives" of hardwired gender that they become almost unrecognizable agents of transformation: "Hormones, humour-like, are produced by light / in order to transform us" (109). For of course, repetition is nonreproductive and always traitorous, and sexuality has everything to do with relationality and pleasure-pain dynamics and very little, if anything at all, to do with some grandiose notion of the incessant spreading of "selfish genes."

As Robertson explains in "Disquiet" (a title that evokes Deleuze's chapter "Perception in the Folds," from which it quotes): "Money, Justice and Gods buy silence. The objects of exchangeability and value can then appear as figures on silence's supporting field, and exchangeability also has its correspondent, communicative sound-objects. From the perspectives of these systems of value and meaning, noise belongs to poverty and the failure of value. Like garbage, it has no meaning at the same time that it signifies an excess of signification; meaning becomes so dense and continuous that it transforms into a field, having previously functioned as figure. In noise, meaning has de-coalesced."[22] This subsong and its relation to gender come into focus in a passage from "The Middle" in a long stanza that begins with the assertion: "I say that I would like philosophy and housework / to frame the beautiful machine that complicates us."[23] Underneath this linkage of philosophy and housework lurks an ecology and habitat that riffs on Deleuze's meditation on Leibniz's baroque fold. In his chapter "The Pleats of Matter," Deleuze imagines Leibniz's fold as a two-story house, which he calls "The Baroque House (an allegory)."[24] On the first story are "common rooms, with 'several small openings': the five senses" and on the second story, a "closed private room, decorated with a drapery diversified by folds, as if it were a living dermis" (*The Fold*, 4–5). Deleuze sees the baroque house in sonic-kinetic alchemical terms: "Leibniz constructs a great Baroque montage that moves between the lower floor, pierced with windows, and the upper floor, blind and closed, but on the other hand resonating as if it were a musical salon translating the visible movements below into sounds up above" (4). Noise is the excluded middle in communications theory, but for Robertson: "Noise is a confusion of figure and field. It presents no discernible figure of meaning. It's not silence's opposite, but an outside, mutating term. In a way, it is the double of silence, with this difference: Silence's indiscernibility is more often institutionally codified and mystified as value—whether spiritual, punitive, or economic."[25]

In the poem "The Middle," in *3 Summers*, Robertson attempts to include the outside by oversaturating the domestic (term, space, time). Deleuze notes, "With Leibniz the curvature of the universe is prolonged according to three other fundamental notions: the fluidity of matter, the elasticity of bodies, and motivating spirit as a mechanism" (4). Robertson's reply to Leibniz and Deleuze is the following:

> If I go home to this one emotion
> in axis inward flung
> to lovingly read obedience
> —with specific improvised spiritual liberty, that is—
>
> I hear weakness speak
> between sexuality and friendship
> in the material bodily lower stratum
> the entire system of degradation and travesty
> the relation to social and historical transformation
> the element of relativity and of becoming
> the extreme difficulty in separating out external compulsion
>   from the experience of desire
> the deafening panting of desire where
> masquerades, orgies, processions, allegories
> dissolved (*3 Summers*, 65)

Instead of being mechanistic, the swerve for Robertson is leaky and (al)chemical: "Hormones, humour-like, are produced by light / in order to unaccountably transform us" (109). Here Robertson draws on the volatile transformative power of these chemical messengers that affect growth and energy flow, among other bodily processes, as well as desire between bodies. This is not de Sade's punishment of the mother's body for the will-to-power of the father in *Philosophy in the Boudoir*. It is its antithesis: here middle-aged women appear in possession of their own desiring bodies, laughing at the homosociality of Lucretius's famous manifesto against sexual desire that ends his book on the sense. Here, Robertson jostles Lucretius's leap from "harmonious motions" from book IV into an acknowledgment of the body's "hormoneous" motions—that is, the revolution waged on the physical by the bio(al)chemical, and the revolution waged on the social by the random as our only given.

However, as Robertson points out, the generative trouble with hormones and the social meaning that we make from their chaotic expressions is that they amplify ambiguity. For example, the same hormonal supplement that people with ovaries are given at menopause to offset some of the effects of aging and change can induce forms of breast cancer. Moreover, Robertson flatly rejects the anthropocentrism that appropriates and territorializes thought as an exclusively human activity:

> When I see the unusually beautiful shapes of fields
> trees scattered at the edges near the road
> there's the path of an idea that's very long and has
>   no edges
> in receding golds and greens
> in the earthly character of thinking (*3 Summers*, 88)

In this passage, from "Rivers," the earth thinks, and the environment is not divided into a system-environment binary but participates in an abundant interspecies process of making-with. Leaves are vestments that gesture toward the internal state (or anima of the tree) but that also signal in a vegetal-social way. As Judith Goldman so beautifully pointed out in her introduction to Robertson's lecture, sumptuary laws of trees are ruled by the seasons—a tree must only wear certain dressings during certain seasons. In "Third Summer," Robertson quips that "in the fashion-nature dialectic / I've positioned myself as the custodian of the inauthentic" (99), a position that emphasizes the processes of becoming rather than fidelity to a platonic ideal.

In each of the poems in *3 Summers*, Robertson seems to be conversing with Lucretius in an undercurrent that shapes the course of thought. For example, Robertson comments on the between-space of the void: "There's been a mystical emptying here so that it's truly empty. / A range of impossibilities opens" (68). These lines come after a meditation about gender, power, language, and poetry, where "every pronoun is absurd" (67), and poetry is "valueless" (67) in the neoliberal marketplace, and therefore circulates on a different ethic of exchange. Klara du Plessis notes: "Rather than pursuing a particular query for the duration of the book, Robertson implies that *3 Summers* is more of a poetic 'grab bag' . . . commissioned for diverse, but often fine arts contexts."[26] I agree with du Plessis that "key words, thought processes, creative involvements and concerns repeat, pulse, loop back an insert themselves persistently into the texts . . . [so that] a book length work comes together to articulate a cohesive, poetic feminism" (16–17). I would add that the currents of continuity—the fluid dynamics that combine various tributaries into a river-like flow— are the dialogic encounters that Robertson orchestrates between her twenty-first century Epicurean feminist reading-writing processes and Lucretius, with Deleuze's investigations of Leibniz and the baroque breaking the binary. Rather than understanding Robertson's feminist Epicurean subsong as supplemental to the ancient poet-physicist, I argue that she is engaging in a process of "making now" that puts her in a poetic field with the likes of Phyllis Webb and that instantiates an *avant-l'esprit, avant-la-lettre* sympoietics that opens the future to its own alterity.

Writing about Webb's poetics, Rob Winger notes:

The only broad parameter upon which contemporary critics seem to agree is that *lyric* is an overqualified term. As Jeffreys notes, almost all contemporary critical approaches to lyric history and contemporary lyric refashioning in the West are, therefore, "productive of paradoxical, meditative, and ambivalent formulations" (xxiii–xxiv) rather than resolved by agreed-upon theories or categories. Webb stresses such paradox, meditation, and ambivalence by engaging Western lyric conventions rather than merely rejecting them, *using* the lyric in order to transform its habits. Rather than motivated by either resistance or response, Webb creates poems of presence to include both. Her poems are not new lyrics so much as they are *now* lyrics.[27]

In a similar way, Robertson motivates the queer (troubadour) spirit of twisting against the seam to thread through the consumerist-present other patterns that may be unrecognizable depending on the lens employed. It is beyond the scope of this essay to catalog the many debates and praises that Robertson stages in her engagement with Lucretius across the eleven poems in *3 Summers,* but they connect Robertson's new materialist feminist poetics to a long tradition of unfixing orthodoxies and thus, to a long tradition of innovative poetics.

"I arrive at the end of nine centuries of rhyme"

I am moved by the question and statement with which Robertson's closes her Creeley Lecture: "Can there be a resuturing of rime? I want to consider the possibility of obedience to a subsong as a collective ethical practice of joyous abundance." Note the French (feminine) spelling of rhyme here in the phrase "a resuturing of rime"; it is a subtle refutation of Western Anglophone lyric's monolingualism and of rhyme as a motor appropriated for masculine ends in both lyric and avant-garde traditions. I feel an uncanny tug as Robertson vividly articulates my own poetic desire to retool poetry and to redistribute poetic value-making processes. Subsong in Robertson's lecture is coded as avian rather than human, switching the power of songwriting from human to bird. There is a deep deterritorialization at work here that goes beyond a single species and embraces an interspecies politics and ethics. As Robertson says: "I don't see that there should be separate words for politics / and nature. / Both are at once free and fixed. They move according to recurrent / attractions" (*3 Summers*, 58). This at a time when our collective creaturely life is under grave threat (we are living inside a mass extinction), and our ability to have our attention attracted by birdsong or the scattering of ants foraging for seeds opens small breathable spaces where we might find an antidote to the deadly meanings foisted upon us by corporate interests. Robertson's hankering for "a collective ethical practice of joyous abundance" resonates with Haraway's conviction that "staying with the trouble requires learning to be truly present, not as a vanishing pivot between awful or edenic pasts and apocalyptic or salvific futures, but as mortal critters entwined in myriad unfinished configurations of places, times, matters and meanings."[28] In reiterating the closing query of Robertson's lecture: "Can there be a resuturing of rime? I want to consider the possibility of obedience to a subsong as a collective ethical practice of joyous abundance," I ask you to consider its reverberation with a question that she poses in the poem "Third Summer": "What if we've made the wrong use of joy of our bodies? What if/ we're to be formal translators of bird cries" (100). To hear the voices of nightingales is to follow a clinamen and shift one's attention towards a subsong. For as Robertson puts it: "I arrive at the end of nine centuries of rhyme / the theatre of value is having its objects slashed" (98).

When I set out to write *Myrmurs: An Exploded Sestina*, Lucretius was far from my mind. Yet the Lucretian gleanings that underpin my work in that book are comparable to those Lucretian traces that the troubadours gathered from Ovid and Virgil—a voltage without a direct touch. Lisa Robertson's poetry and essays were on my mind—in particular, *Lisa Robertson's Magenta Soul Whip*, which bears on its (color-complementary) mustard cover, silver embossed letters.[29] Here, the letter *o* of the word *Soul* on this cover is an emphasized (by several circlings) *trou*, similar to the hole she describes finding in the gutter of the ninth-century codex containing *De rerum natura, Vossianus Oblongus*:

> In the facsimile *Oblongus* codex at the bottom margin on the page containing lines 1140–1159 of the fourth book, I saw what at first appeared to be the photographed image of a small oval hole about the size and shape of my thumbnail, tidy cut from the vellum of the original. Bordering this ellipse, I saw a faint drawing that added a labial ornamental border around the shape. It seemed that some sort of monkish pornographic doodle had been censored. At closer examination I realized that the elliptical absence had in fact not been cut from the page by some historical censor; it was a flaw inherent in the structure of the vellum—the trace of an animal's wound perhaps. Several of these photographed images of material *mise-en-abîmes* appeared as I leafed through the codex. In each instance, the page was cut from the larger skin so that the scar found its place in a margin, so as not to interfere with the scribe's work. But here in book four, the scribe had decorated the flaw in the skin with this mildly and endearingly erotic doodle. The tiny absence was animated: a lacework.[30]

Robertson's acute attention to sensual detail extends to the Early Modern translation history of Lucretius's poem, indexing not only a multilingual textual inheritance but also an interspecies sympoietics. The vellum upon which Lucretius's text is preserved (precariously so) enacts an animal-human textual interrelationship. This recalls the numerous communications contexts of sympoiesis that Haraway evokes in *Staying with the Trouble*: "*Sympoiesis* is a simple word; it means 'making-with.' Nothing makes itself; nothing is really autopoietic or self-organizing . . . *Sympoiesis* is a word proper to complex, dynamic, responsive, situated, historical systems. It is a word for worlding-with, in company. Sympoiesis enfolds autopoiesis and generatively unfurls and extends it" (58). The transmission history of medieval textuality was animated by the animal skins upon which it was written and preserved. Without interspecies parasitism, manuscript preservation as we know it in the Western tradition would not have been possible. The dead cellular surface of vellum provided a crucial surface for coding and recoding. Haraway's work over the decades has been to demonstrate and persuade us that our writing technologies and our technologies of self-making (autopoiesis) are not innocent, in spite of what Christian origin stories promulgate. Yet what makes sympoiesis such a compelling concept is its complicity in all systems of meaning-making and their inherent violence. In her exploration of the erotic encoding of an "animal wound," Robertson participates in the non-innocent textual economy (one might even say taxidermy) that allows a vital current of thought and desire to pass from the ninth century to the twenty-first. In her essay on Lucretius, she animates reading as a subspace in the BDSM mode of alternative state of consciousness achieved by constraint or excesses of pain-pleasure in which the subjected falls in and out of ordinary time in the pursuit of pleasure. Thus, she links contemporary nonreproductive erotic practices with Lucretius: "The poem is a hormone" (*3 Summers*, 11). By sticking with the pleasure of the "middle" of life (that which falls between the horizon events of birth and death), Robertson evades the instrumentalist story lines of the "selfish gene" fetishized by the sociobiologists, such as E. O. Wilson, and all the attendant binary expectations of behavior and gender performance.

In Robertson's poem called "The Middle," we find three stanzas that speak directly to the trouble of staying with the pleasure as a second sex/gender:

This year I am sick of language
cut radiant gentle and frank
little angle of dissolved rhyme
who sires the flagrant exemplum
what if language is the suppression
of vitalist vocal co-movement
by the military-industrial complex?
What if language is the market
Now their body gestures
now their body conducts
which isn't changing the body itself
it's only changing the activity of their body
but it's also changing the body
like a sensitive shrub with eyes and blood
its act is precious form
otherwise known as rhyme
and it is no good and I continue
leaning on the tree for rest.
I call this the immaterial material
Its cosmological fluttering, its infrared infinitude
refuses dumbed-down instrumentality.
Its scale is a world (70–71)

Taking up a favorite theme of Lucretius's in the final stanza, Robertson innovates the invisible-indivisible. Meanwhile, the difference and contiguity that Robertson finds between bodily capacities to

engage in the world—bodies that gesture and bodies that con-
duct—speak to her welding together of vitalist and materialist
traditions; traditions that have often been framed as being in
competition. For Robertson, gesture (that is, material semiotics)
or the meaning-making dynamics of the body's surfaces are but
one mode (Deleuze and Guattari call this a "molar" form), and
the body's conduction of vital energy (what Deleuze and Guattari
call a "molecular" form) produce two different contingencies
for a body.[31] Before and beyond the spirit of the times, before
and beyond the language that screens it, there are multilayered,
generative processes of making-with that refuse instrumental-
izations—such as the endless accumulation and reproduction of
prefabricated meanings and relations—and instead work in favor
of newly attempted connections, however provisional.

These dialogic poetics lead to a widening of sensual awareness, as Robertson proposes by instantiating a feedback loop
between the troubadours writing in the Occitan language and
her own poetry: "The presence of birds—via birdsong and also
bird speech, where song and speech seem undifferentiated—is a
commonplace in these first authored vernacular poems on the
European continent . . . [The birds] are in dialogue with poets.
For poets and birds, as the season or the time is new, . . . so is
the song, the speech, the desire. This newness is an effect of the
surprise of temporal difference in repetition expressed so vividly
by means of the then-new compositional technique called rhyme."
These dynamics of interspecies dialogue and rhyme (making cor-
respondences of sound) structure what Robertson calls "subsong,"
bringing a thicket of secular medieval poetics and politics into
a twenty-first-century poetic event. In tracking the possibilities
opened by the quality and textualization of sweetness in birdsong,
from Occitan language poetry into the troubling soundscape of
a planet in the throes of mass genocide and mass multispecies
extinction, Robertson evokes synesthesia: a sound becomes a
taste, and the ear spreads a banquet on the tongue. Sound's fre-

quencies are interrupted and redistributed by the tongue's reach for new collations.

Taste itself is a complex sense that calls upon smell, too. Like tasting, the act of smelling involves hosting strange particles within the intimate folds of the face. As Robertson bluntly puts it in a poem called "On Form": "the earlobe there is a bony poppy / fucking wildly at the edge of capital" (*3 Summers*, 37) and, further, "the ear is also a hive it produces / wax which is a humor it is the nest / of a swallow" (37–38). Gustation as a poetic gesture is a rope that slips very slyly into "guest"-ation, or that making-strange beloved of modernisms, but coated in a-hospitable bacterial time. The sinuses dump into the mouth and confound the boundaries between living system and environment as well as between bodies. The throat hosts voice and song, the gesture of swallowing (as abrupt admittance of outside in), and is also a muster point for bodily humors. When a birdsong slips into a sweetness on the tongue in Robertson's poetics, the process of synesthesia allows an interspecies intimacy to take place, one that refuses the old hierarchies of patriarchal fantasy in which "man" dominates all other earthly creatures. Robertson ushers forth the spirit of renovating letters in a mode that "refuses dumbed-down instrumentality" (*3 Summers*, 71).

Gilles Deleuze and Félix Guattari argued for a "line of flight" away from biopolitical management that could be thought of (poetically) as an alchemical process where a being is transformed in stages into a becoming: becoming-intense, becoming-woman, becoming-animal, becoming-imperceptible. Now, corporate social media players such as Twitter (now called X) seem to have reversed those stages to ensure that global consumers are stuck in their being-user role, where authority and power are evacuated from online speech, so that instead of opening realms of possibility in the process becoming-read-as-animal, the user-being is robbed of the richness of possibility while also being impoverished in actualization. In "In the Beginning Was the Word: The Genesis of

Biological Theory," Haraway insists that what comes to count as a unit of meaning is as much about the power dynamics inherent in processes of meaning-making as it is about who is recognized as having the authority to speak and be believed (a process of mastery).[32] Although poets and scientists are accorded asymmetrical meaning-making powers, poets do still work in words, and as Charles Bernstein maintained, "Poetry is the research and development branch of language."[33] For Robertson, nightingales offer us a different temporality. If bird and bug "voices" (those of nightingales and ants, for instance) are among those slated for the category of "noise" in dominant culture, then attuning our ear to their subsongs would change the rhythm of our lines. These concerns shape Robertson's approach to rethinking poetic tools for a twenty-first century making-with poetics and poetry: "The quality called 'newness' or 'innovation,' still a core value and problem within contemporary avant-gardes, also inaugurated that earlier avant-garde secular verse culture, the one called 'troubadour.' In the eleventh century, the new poetry announces itself in community with birds, who sing, claims William IX of Aquitaine in his poem 'Segon lo vers de novel chan,' ('On the model of the new rime,' my translation). Poets and birds learn from one another, take each other as masters." Thus, mastery as a concept is folded over itself, with birds as our hosts, and in asynchronic (as opposed to diachronic) time, through which Robertson evokes the sweetness of revolt. In her return to troubadour poetics with a contemporary twist and with many questions, and in her turn away from reductive modernisms towards a process of making-with, Robertson breaks open a Poetics of Endangerment, not to further fetishize the diminishing flocks of nightingales in the French countryside where she lives but rather to endanger the Western concepts that enable their destruction, "as in the non-abstract frequency-receiving gesture of beginning" (*3 Summers*, 78).

We overlap, as poets, in our desire to find alternative materialist fields of thought and practice. We overlap in seeking out medieval poets with whom to converse and argue. Although Robertson's feminist Epicureanism is overt and mine is latent in my poetry so far, my work does obey the swerve—radical difference (and singularity) as a structuring principle of the universe—and the desire to make new poetic tools. My creative research begins from the premise that poetry—when it is working—makes visible and/or audible the dynamics—that is, the forces, powers, affects—that structure our lives as individuals and as collectivities. I don't mean to suggest that poetry offers us an unmediated access to some notion of "reality," but rather that even the most semantically opaque (even asemic) poetry stages, frames, and distills the intensities and microdynamics that shape us. In doing so, poetry allows structures of various scales and registers to touch and collide, to vibrate and to be felt in the body. What emerges from those encounters is the matter of poetry.

In *Myrmurs: An Exploded Sestina* (2015) I deconstruct Western categories of gender, race, and species. I live as an unruly subject of Western categories, and in contest with Western thought's insistence on an inanimate, hierarchically structured universe—premises that I refuse in my writing. Rather than focusing on a particular source text, *Myrmurs* focuses on a specific medieval form: the sestina. The twelfth-century troubadour Arnaut Daniel de Riberac is widely credited with the form's invention. An erotic form that investigates desire by means of linguistic constraint, the sestina, with its pattern of repeated end-words, could be conceived as a machine of cumulative affect whose motor is echo. Catherine E. Wall elaborates upon what she sees as the normative effects of the sestina as a genre that works through obsession, repetition, and affirmation toward "a singular aesthetic goal."[34] My intention in working with the sestina was to open a closed form by extending its macrostructures to add complexity to its microstructures; thus, the aesthetic goals are dynamic and various in my hands.

Perhaps the three most commented upon aspects of the sestina are: its sixes: six stanzas, end words, and lines in regular stanzas; its envoi: that special seventh stanza in which end words are doubled up in the lines, and the number of lines is cut in half; and its retrograde-cross pattern of end-word repetition. The echo as a concept marks the crossing between stanzas: words become unfaithful to themselves by repetition. In *Bodies That Matter*, Judith Butler claims: "The future of the signifier of identity can only be secured through a repetition that fails to repeat loyally, a reciting of the signifier that must commit a disloyalty against identity—a catachresis—in order to secure its future, a disloyalty that works the iterability of the signifier for what remains non-self-identical in any invocation of identity, namely, the iterable or temporal conditions of its own possibility."[35] At this point in Butler's argument, the ritual repetition, in this case of a name or more precisely a "lost and improper referent" (218), is key in the production of gender norms that in turn construct the materiality of sex. This required rearticulation forces the referent to come up against its porosity. In order to have a future, a referent must not echo into dissipation, but reply to itself, thus reasserting itself *through difference* by adapting to its ever-changing context. This transformative re-citation is also the engine that drives the sestina as a form. The six repeated words act as names that produce the identity of the sestina. Yet for the poem to be able to continue and for the end word to be able to repeat, the context must shift significantly to accommodate—not an echo, but an adaptation. The constitutive constraint (to recite Butler's phrase) of *Myrmurs* is the adherence of the pattern of repetition typical of the sestina where the function of end word was transferred to the domain of the title and the function of line was transferred to the domain of poem. The book is one long sestina, six intertwined poems that interact with and change each other: "Noise," "Letters," "Pleasure," "Crowd," "Volume," "Incorrigible." This book-length structure is what I call an "exploded sestina."

A sestina needs an obsession. I became enamored with ants and myrmecological writing about the same time as I sat down to work on the exploded sestina; ants began to appear at all levels of the poem. It was uncanny for me to read Haraway's *Staying with the Trouble,* published the year after my book *Myrmurs,* in that she devotes a chapter to ants, specifically taking up Deborah Gordon's work on harvester ants at Stanford.[36] We were both reading Gordon and thinking about mutualisms and parasitisms and language! *Myrmurs*'s poems employ various colliding vocabularies, such as those of myrmecology and fluid dynamics, lavender linguistics, and flapper slang. The extended metaphorical conceit is that the ants disperse these vocabularies, bringing the poems into contact and affecting their structures. For example, the poem "Pleasure" changes forms and vocabularies about halfway through—it goes from a surrealist narrative line that drifts between wakefulness and dream, to an eight-line acrostic with imagist proclivities built around the name "Eurydice." This transformation happens on account of the interactions that it has with the other poems—which is possible only because of the ants. I work with language here as a self-organizing system (or, since reading Haraway, perhaps it would be better to say a sympoietic system), and all of the themes emerge from these structural aspects.

The question of what effects contemporary Western (read neoliberal) categories of gender and species produce and foreclose at the level of individual bodies and of populations is answered in a number of ways in *Myrmurs,* even as the book attempts to enact forms of resistance to neocolonial structures through the metaphorical jaws of ants. Throughout, the subject of whatever poem is never allowed to be alone, but is always forced into relation with nonhuman collectivities. This is not a recuperative gesture, but rather, a disruptive one.

Poets like Robertson and scholars like Haraway are working against the grain of the Neoplatonic, Cartesian, sociobiological inheritance of domination and instrumentalization with its anthropocentrism and are instead insisting on the improvisatory pleasure of the body as vibratory instrument and on the significance of the middle of the story: everything that comes between birth and death and especially of the coproduction of communicative and relational values, for example in the elations of birdsong.

Notes

1. Here I am using Lucy Hutchinson's mid-seventeenth century translation, which Robertson quotes in her essay "Lastingness: Réage, Lucrèce, Arendt," in *Nilling: Prose Essays On Noise, Pornography, The Codex, Melancholy, Lucretius, Folds, Cities and Related Aporias* (Toronto: Book*Hug, 2012), 37–38. Robertson notes that, "Hutchinson's translation of the invocation . . . is the most beautiful English version that I have read" (37). I have also consulted Lucretius, *The Nature of Things,* trans., with notes by, A. E. Stallings (London and New York: Penguin Classics, 2007), 3.

2. Robertson, "Lastingness: Réage, Lucrèce, Arendt," 35.

3. Robertson, 37–38.

4. Lisa Robertson, *3 Summers* (Toronto: Coach House Books, 2016), 58.

5. "Noise" is a concept that Robertson has written eloquently about in her essay "Disquiet," *Nilling,* 55–70.

6. Anonymous, "troubadour," *Online Etymology Dictionary.* Last accessed April 12, 2020, https://www.etymonline.com/word/troubadour.

7. Phyllis Webb, "There *Are* the Poems," in *Peacock Blue: The Collected Poems,* ed. John F. Hulcoop (Vancover: Talonbooks, 2014), 405.

8. Henri Bergson, *Creative Evolution,* trans. Arthur Mitchell (New York: Modern Library, 1944), 58; cited in Elizabeth Grosz, *The Nick of Time: Politics, Evolution, and the Untimely* (Durham and London: Duke University Press, 2004), 244.

9. Robertson, *3 Summers.*

10. Ryan J. Johnson, *The Deleuze-Lucretius Encounter* (Edinburgh: Edinburgh University Press, 2017), 3.

11. Elizabeth Grosz, *Time Travels: Feminism, Nature, Power* (Durham and London: Duke University Press, 2005), 152.

12. Donna Haraway, *Staying with the Trouble: Making Kin in the Chthulucene* (Durham and London: Duke University Press, 2016).

13. Sina Queyras, "Sapere Aude: On '3 Summers' and the Poetry of Lisa Robertson," *Los Angeles Review of Books,* February 2, 2017, https://lareviewofbooks.org/article/sapere-aude-on-3-summers-and-the-poetry-of-lisa-robertson/.

14. Stacy Doris, *Knot* (Athens: University of Georgia Press, 2006), no page given; cited in *Nilling*, v.

15. "Acknowledgements," *Nilling*, 90.

16. Robertson, "Lastingness: Réage, Lucrèce, Arendt," 24.

17. Shannon Maguire, *Myrmurs: An Exploded Sestina* (Toronto: Book*hug Press, 2015).

18. Angela Carter, *The Sadeian Woman: An Exercise in Cultural History* (London: Virago Press, 2000), 24.

19. Robertson, "Disquiet," 61, 70.

20. Robertson, "Disquiet," 65.

21. Lucretius, book IV: "The Senses," *The Nature of Things*, trans. by A. E. Stallings, introduction by Richard Jenkyns (London and New York, Penguin Classics, 2007), 107.

22. Gilles Deleuze, *The Fold: Leibniz and the Baroque*, trans. and foreword by Tom Conley (Minneapolis: University of Minnesota Press, 1993), 87; cited in Robertson, "Disquiet," 63.

23. *3 Summers*, 67.

24. Deleuze, *The Fold*, 5.

25. Robertson, "Disquiet," 63.

26. Klara du Plessis, "in hormonal forest," *Unfurl: Four Essays* (Montreal: Gaspereau Press, 2019), 16.

27. Rob Winger, "How to Know Now: 'Zen' Poetics in Phyllis Webb's *Naked Poems* and *Water and Light*," *Studies in Canadian Literature/Études En littérature Canadienne* 35, no. 2 (2010): 9. Mark Jeffreys, "Lyric Poetry and the Resistance to History," *New Definitions of Lyric: Theory, Technology, and Culture*, ed. Mark Jeffreys (New York: Garland, 1998), ix–xxiv.

28. Donna Haraway, *Staying with the Trouble*, 1.

29. Lisa Robertson, *Lisa Robertson's Magenta Soul Whip* (Toronto: Coach House, 2009).

30. Robertson, "Lastingness: Réage, Lucrèce, Arendt," 21–22.

31. Gilles Deleuze and Félix Guattari, *A Thousand Plateaus: Capitalism and Schizophrenia*, trans. Brian Massumi (Minneapolis: University of Minnesota Press, 1987), 277–279.

32. Donna J. Haraway, "In the Beginning Was the Word: The Genesis of Biological Theory," *Signs* 6.3 (1981), 469–481.

33. Charles Bernstein, "On Poetry, Language, and Teaching: A Conversation with Charles Bernstein," *boundary 2* 23, no. 3 (Autumn 1996), 45–66.

34. Catherine E. Wall, "Bilingualism and Identity in Julia Alvarez's Poem 'Bilingual Sestina,'" *MELUS* 28, no. 4 (Winter, 2003), 133.

35. Judith Butler, *Bodies That Matter: On the Discursive Limits of Sex* (New York: Routledge, 1993), 220.

36. Deborah Gordon et al., "Colony Variation in the Collective Regulation of Foraging by Harvester Ants," *Behavioral Ecology* 22, no. 2 (2011), 429–435.

Chapter 6

2018 Robert Creeley Lecture Roundtable Discussion[1]

Featuring Lisa Robertson, with Shannon Maguire and Liz Howard

MODERATED BY JUDITH GOLDMAN

Poetry Collection, University at Buffalo

FRIDAY, APRIL 13, 2018

Judith Goldman: We're going to get started. First of all, thank you so much for being here, and thank you to Jim Maynard, who is the curator of the Special Collections, and to the library staff for hosting us here today. We're really grateful to you and [for] your generosity always to Poetics.

I'm going to explain very briefly how this afternoon will unfold. First, you will have presentations from Shannon and Liz, just brief statements that are responding to Lisa's lecture, perhaps connecting that lecture up with their own work and their own practice, and any other issues that they care to introduce. Lisa will then respond, and we'll have some conversation up front here, probably for a few go-rounds, and then we'd like to invite you to join in. I'll come back up here and moderate. If you'd like to speak, include yourself. If it seems like there's a space and you can just say something, you can do that. If you need to raise your hand, that's okay, too—however you want to join in. We want it to be conversation for all of us here. Let's get started.

Shannon Maguire: Thank you, Judith, and thank you also to Myung, and to all of the organizers. It's been absolutely fabulous, and everybody's been very friendly and welcoming, so I really appreciate that. I wanted to say, before I respond to Lisa's lecture, and before I connect that to some of the work that I'm doing, that, Judith, the phrases you had in your intro yesterday, "the vegetal sumptuary" and "vegetal eros," have really stuck with me, and I think I'm going to come back to that—not only when I'm discussing Lisa's lecture, but also when I'm talking about my work with ants in my sestina, and so on.

One of my goals here in my response to Lisa's lecture is to come back, return or refrain, to some of the ideas and concepts and questions that Lisa brought out yesterday, and ask you to think further about certain things as well, or to look at them again. Of course, the central idea of the refrain is a cut or a break, and rhyme, too, as you know, almost being somehow related tangentially to a broken tongue, which came out in the lecture yesterday, also resonates, with the idea of a break or a cut. Or (I'm even thinking ahead [to my paper]) I read a lot of Elizabeth Grosz; for instance, I'm thinking of *The Nick of Time*, which came out in about 2004—and there's an idea there that it's possible to create little nicks in historical time in such a way that all of a sudden the future [of that past] becomes unpredictable. And that seemed to resonate really well with what you're doing. I think, as well, the idea that it's the voice of the latin of birds, or the voice of the bird, or the sonic-scape of the interspecies connection, [the] vocal and oral connection between nightingales and poets, adds an interesting dimension to that idea of nick or break, and the beak is maybe something that can prick some of this huge historic time. I think one of the issues that this work is dealing with, even if it isn't apparent right away, is the problem we're facing right now with our systems of communications. We're living in an age of Twitter, where it's often hard to actually have dialogues or conversations, so the idea of actually inhabiting an environment, a small space, and finding ways of improvising across latins, as Lisa calls it, I think is really political, and it's important. It's that idea of the bird voice: the multiple kinds of love that that bird voice can carry is a really powerful thing to think about in our age. I chose Twitter as the social media to pick on for obvious reasons, but that edge-work rhyme that Lisa described yesterday is a way of breaking, so I wanted us to talk a little bit further about that, and also the deferral, too.

One of the sentences that really jumped out to me as I was listening to the lecture last night was, "Rhymes are social facts, and they are structures of memory," so the site of rhymes being structures of memory is another thing that I want to talk a little bit more about—and that was connected to the moment when you [Lisa] said, "Love is the opposite of force; rhyme is the opposite of force." The idea that you link that to *joi*—"composition as a distributed active happiness" and the idea of obedience to a sub-song—I want to hear more about subsongs and that relationship between the subsong and the person who is serving it, and what that can do politically. Those are some of the questions I walked out of the lecture with, and I'm going to connect them a little bit to the poetics that I'm engaged in, because this is an amazing chance to sit here and have a conversation.

I've been working with medieval vernaculars in my poetry for some time now. I'm just on my third book doing that right now. My own creative research begins from the premise that poetry, when it's working, makes visible, and or audible, the dynamics—

that is, the forces and powers and affects—that structure our lives as individuals and collectivities, so that idea of rhyme being a structure of memory is linked up to that.

[Maguire here delivered an earlier version of their response essay (see chapter 5 of this volume). Howard's remarks, improvised from handwritten notes and based on previous correspondence among the three participants about the event and Robertson's lecture, followed.]

Liz Howard: Thank you, Shannon. I just have some brief remarks that draw on a few aspects of Lisa's talk that I found particularly interesting as regards my own practice. I wanted to open up with a particularly striking image that I believe you [Lisa] opened up with early on in our email exchanges, or how you initially framed this talk, which was the image of Philomela's tongue, severed tongue, stuttering in the earth, which is an image that has haunted me—because it is the presence or part of the body that is still trying to speak. It's still somehow animate, but it's this entropic remainder that is nevertheless nutritive: it's returning to the soil. And then, also (another thing in my essential nature is goth, there's no avoiding it) there is the Albigensian genocide, where twenty thousand people were slaughtered in a day or two days. I'm just thinking of that sort of bloodshed. There's no way of having that sort of bloodshed being separate from your fields, for example.

Lisa Robertson: Like agricultural fields.

Liz: Right, so for me, I'm very much interested in this notion of the return, of the refrain, insofar as there is this odd eruption of the new through trauma, and the sort of transformational element of it. We have [Philomela] transforming into the nightingale, and the irony of being transformed into a creature that can't help but sing, that can't help but tell. And then the notion of the return in the refrain with survival, and with a certain notion of survivance.

Gerald Vizenor, Ojibwe scholar, has this notion of survivance, the continuance of being, powered through storytelling, and not just through a kind of identification with victim codes or being labeled as a victim. I'm still thinking my way through this really powerful sentence from French theorist Catherine Malabou, who works at the intersection of psychoanalysis, philosophy, and neuroscience. In her work *Ontology of the Accident*, she writes, "Out of a deep cut in a biography, a new being emerges for the second time." There's this—kind of related to what you wrote, it's all innovation, citational. It's interesting, "a new being emerges for a second time" . . . I'm still wrapping my head around that. There's also what this Ojibwe poet and scholar, Leanne Simpson, writes about resurgence. A resurgence that's essentially tied to land and presence, Indigenous presence, on the land and through song, ritual. That brings me through to my own practice.

My book is called *Infinite Citizen of the Shaking Tent*. The shaking tent, in Ojibwe, is called *jiisakaan*. It's a sacred, oracular Ojibwe practice, and I feel as though there's a connection there, with divination, the receiving of song, receiving of voice as, in this ceremony, voices are essentially consulted. What happens in the ceremony is there is a conjuror, a specific individual who is a practitioner of the rite, a *jiisakiiwinini*, and they are commissioned for this rite by a community member, who needs information about the future: where best to go hunting, where best to travel to avoid foes, to inquire about the health of a relative who's at some distance away. And this conjuror will construct a tent of specific materials and dimensions, and inside this tent, spirits, who are distributed in time and space, *manidoog*, animal-affiliated spirits, will come and speak to a central spirit, Mikinaak, a turtle spirit, who acts as a translator. The *manidoog* all speak their own specific languages, and Mikinaak is the only spirit who speaks Ojibwe or Anishinaabemowin, and Mikinaak speaks in translation directly to the conjuror who then delivers the desired information to the community.

[I've only] read about this practice—I've never witnessed it for myself, because there's just been a radical disintegration of family and practice due to colonization and the assimilative mission of government and church, which essentially continues to be active in Canada. For example, in my family history and insofar as I can trace back genealogically, the first record of my native family shows up in the early 1700s, of a distant great-grandfather, the father of a son who was baptized by a Jesuit missionary. And then from there Ojibwe names begin to disappear, replaced by French names—usually the name of the priest that baptized them—and, of course, my grandmother was the last speaker of Ojibwe . . . I never really knew her. She taught my aunt some words, so I have to teach all of this to myself. It's an innovation, the innovation is a choice for me, in how I pull what I know of the traditional world through an experimental, feminist poetics. It's a reclamation: the resurgence in this giving to myself. It's the reemergence of the previous.

When I read about this practice, I found myself identifying with this role of the conjuror, because I feel as though this is very much what is happening when I am writing poetry . . . This sounds very *woo-woo*, right? But I have a sense as though I'm taking in information, and I often write in this sort of stream of consciousness or automatic writing type of style. I just write solid blocks of texts, and I will go and refine or read or perform a translation kind of procedure, and form these weird poems out of that, so I really creatively identify with the *jiisakaan*, shaking tent procedure.

I wanted to close with an odd, synchronicity-type thing around Twitter, things that I re-tweeted. One really cool thing that I re-tweeted . . . I follow this account called Women's Art, and they tweeted this incredible photo—anyone who wants to see it after, I'll show it to you—it's this incredible linen jacket, worn by this woman named Agnes Richter, who was a seamstress, who was forced into an Austrian asylum during the late 1800s, and she embroidered her life story onto this jacket as an attempt to regain her identity. So, it's very much the same as Philomela weaving her account into this garment and sending it to her sister, that kind of soft architecture. . .

Lisa: Threadiness. . .

Liz: Yeah, threadiness of women laying down their account in this way. That's something to talk about. And then, also, something that's another part of my life, working in memory research, in neuroscience. I tweeted this quote by Jacques Roubaud—whom I recently started to get into—regarding this one compositional strategy that he started using when he was writing his book *The Loop*. It illustrates how memory is a destructive, reconstructive process. Again, this eruption of the new through destruction, this rhyming, this returning of "me." How he would find this memory of childhood, and he would try to write it and rewrite it over and over again, until at some point he discovered that what he could remember was no longer the original memory. What he could remember was only what he had written, the episodic act of writing itself, and he said, "By this way I destroyed my memory," which sounds horrific. It sounds horrifically beautiful. It's used to destroy the original memory, but you form a new memory. There's this notion of writing as a return with difference. A new being emerges for a second time. Those are my remarks.

Lisa: Obviously, there's not a way for me to fully respond to Liz's and Shannon's extremely rich, evocative, and provocative remarks and presentations of their own thinking, so I've been scrawling notes like mad on these little cards, which now I have in front of me. I have little snatches, phrases, that hopefully I can speak towards and from.

Shannon, you asked me to say something more about sub-songs, so I thought I would use that specific question as a way in and see where that takes us. I'm going to give a little bit of background on that term. It's my riff on a term from Roland Barthes's "The Grain of the Voice." In "The Grain of the Voice," which was a 1972 essay, he talks at some length about Julia Kristeva's work *Desire in Language*. Now, I confess I have not read Julia Kristeva's *Desire in Language*. I am at the age of fifty-seven beginning to read Julia Kristeva, so I am absolutely no kind of . . . I cannot represent Julia Kristeva. But what Barthes said about Kristeva was that she spoke about two levels of language's textuality: the geno-text and the pheno-text. Barthes took up Kristeva's idea of the geno-text, but called it geno-song. What this geno-/pheno- level binary structure is about is Kristeva's take on conscious, instrumental language-use, which follows normative syntax and syntagmatic construction, and which she calls a pheno-text, and then the more subconscious or unconscious level in which meaning is circulating beneath the level of the pheno-text, giving different information that sometimes goes against the grain of normative utilitarian language. She calls that the geno-text.

Barthes takes Julia Kristeva's binary description of two kinds of meaning-making going on simultaneously in language, and he brings it into his analysis of song. He's talking about musical performance, and he discusses different recordings of German *Lieder*. For him, geno-song is this corporality—which is different from virtuosity and technique, the learned aspect of vocal production—this corporality that's arising unbidden into a vocal production, that's bringing the texture, in his thinking—perversity, desire, heresy—into the voice. So he's appropriating Julia Kristeva, and then I in turn appropriate Barthes. Instead of calling it geno-song, I call it the subsong. [*Subsong* is a term from ornithology, referring to nonterritorial birdsong.] I was thinking of this subsong as song's otherness—the other thinking, the other corporality that rhyme is presenting to us under the surface of the text.

I'm really interested in the idea of geno-song or subsong partly in relationship to thinking and learning I've been doing about Émile Benveniste's late writing. He's a French linguist who died in 1976, and began working in the '30s. His late work, which was unachieved but recently published in the form of transcribed notes, was going to be a major book on Baudelaire's poetic language. Benveniste was interested in how poetry becomes . . . how meaning in language moves differently in poetry than it does in the account of meaning-making that comes from Saussure's structuralist description of the sign as the binary unit of language. Benveniste talks about the phrase as the unit of language. When he says the phrase, he means groups and clusterings of words and how sound, echo, subrational association, all kinds of linguistic events, which are not part of the sign, are actually making the meaning of the poetry. It felt familiar to me. It was interesting to hear a linguist trained in historical, comparative, and structuralist methods taking poetry not as a special marginal case of language, but as an example of how the core of language works. So, for Benveniste, the reason why poetry was interesting was not as an example of a special aestheticized subset of language. It's performing a work in language and consciousness which we are performing also in our in our quotidian conversations, in our basic experience with language.

I loved that Benveniste put poetry at the center of a theory of how meaning moves in language—because to me it seems precise to say that poetry is at the center of language. I was really interested in Caroline Dinshaw, whom you brought up Shannon, and the idea of the "amateur" reader. Because it seems to me that in a certain way, all of us here, to various degrees, we're professionalized. Our language use vis-à-vis poetry is professionalized. We're in this institutional space because we received a certain training, or we've ridden on the coattails of certain training, in my instance. I've just tried to ride on Steve McCaffery's coattails. But to think of this idea of an amateurism as being the core of what poetry is, rather than it being a specialized outside activity . . . I mean, my mother always wants to know—now that she's finally accepted that I'm a poet—she wants to know where I got it from. Did I get it from my grandmother? And the thing is, my grandma wrote maybe three occasional poems in her life—about the football coach's retirement, a walnut tree being cut down on their street, and so forth. It's got nothing to do with grandma.

But, in fact, we do make up poems, right? You know when you used to say, "Oh, I made up a poem," rather than, "I have become a poet because my book has been published and so forth," and to think of this primary activity as a way of giving language, shaping language to give to one another and understanding that the subsong of language is something that is at the core of our experience of community. It seems really, really important to me.

Liz, you begin by talking about this fabulous word *nutritive*, about the severed tongue having a nutritive function, of leaking its blood into the ground, and the relationship of this leaked blood of the severed tongue to agricultural fields and our field of poetry. We are continually eating the severance of our cultural memory, and that is the subsong that we are speaking in spite of ourselves, or not quite speaking because we're stuttering it. Or we're terribly anxious because part of us doesn't think we deserve the position we've been given. I used to, when I was giving a reading, very often start to cry in the middle of public reading—my voice would stop and some different vocal thing would start coming that was not the vocal thing that I wished for, not by any means whatsoever. This presence of a nonvolitional texture, which is giving us information about ways we are in community, in spite of the institutional formations given to us—by capital, by colonial administration, etc.—is something that feels very important to me. None of this is quite connecting, but I feel a lot of enthusiasm about what I'm hearing from you.

[The roundtable took a brief pause here.]

Lisa: I wanted to mention Leanne Simpson. She's a writer from Southern Ontario, whose family is Anishinaabe. She wrote a book called *Dancing on Our Turtle's Back,* which is a collection of critical essays about her reentering the conceptual field of Anishinaabe culture, by going to elders and learning the language. She would go to four different elders to learn one word, one conceptual term, and she'd get different takes on it, and this is how she got her doctorate—using traditional intellectual practices. It's just so great. Within Leanne Simpson's telling of her study in the conceptual field of Anishinaabe culture, she talks about a story that she heard from an elder about how the Anishinaabe people decided, many generations ago, to respond to the arrival of the colonists in Atlantic Canada. She says that the Anishinaabe people—their original territory was in what is now Nova Scotia . . . Basically, as the British and the French started arriving, they realized that they were in deep shit, and they had to make a plan for how to survive . . . How to survive the invasion and the genocide. She said that the Anishinaabe elders made a five-hundred-year plan. I was really incredibly moved by this statement. "Okay, let's make a five-hundred-year plan." Part of the plan was to split into different groups and scatter in different directions, with the idea that many groups were going to be killed or assimilated, but some threads would survive. So this five-hundred-year plan was to divide and scatter. This is what I recalled from my reading of the book, which was about two years ago.

One thing I wanted to bring in from Leanne's story is the question of duration, this long duration. How in our thinking of newness, how the relevance and the necessity of entering, of thinking the long duration, is necessary in order for us to take responsibility for our own continuance. And for some of us to take responsibility for our ancestral participation in acts of force and aggression. A deep past is speaking through our throats, which may be closing when we don't wish for them to close. I think this is something that you were talking about, Shannon, that this kind of pleating of a long duration into the experience of newness is part of a queering or a feminist opening of the work of time in language, and you named such really important people: Caroline Bergvall, Angela Carr, Erín Moure, and I would add Catriona Strang, who wrote really fabulous *Carmina Burana* translations in the early '90s. There's been a wonderful presence of feminist, experimental thinkers working in the field of the medieval . . . For me, this interest in looking at the political, cultural, social history happening in the Aquitaine area, a thousand years ago now—it's twelve hundred to eight hundred years ago—is very much of the present. [I live in this region.]

The more I learned about the actions of the Pope and the Crown and the Church on what was an extremely secular and/or heretical culture, the more bells rang for me in terms of what I've been very slowly learning about colonial histories and genocides of Indigenous peoples in Canada. I felt that as I was reading and learning, I was watching a before-echo of something that happened on this continent about five hundred years after that. I was feeling that the colonial appropriation of new world territories, and genocides of the peoples of these territories, was an extension of what I was already witnessing in this medieval formation of the concept of Europe as a pure and boundaried space. My experience of living in Europe is, as is many people's, inflected right now with the fact that the Mediterranean has become a mass grave. Europe continues to inscribe a border between North and South, continues to deny the historical presence of Arab people and their thinking, from around the year 700 to 1400, within what is now considered to be the European continent. They can deny this Arab presence, this polylingual co-forming of an extremely diverse culture which still exists as a subculture. They can deny the fact that the Mediterranean Sea, which used to be a fertile basin of cultural exchange, a polysemic explosion of variation—sharing and translating and transcribing of philosophy, of song, of craft, of art . . . They've turned the rich basin of the Mediterranean literally into a mass grave. People's names disappear on a daily basis. People's names sink into this sea. We don't know the names or the numbers of Southern hemisphere migrants. We don't know how many of them are in the sea.

So living in Europe now is very much about rethinking and finding ways to understand and meaningfully perceive and resist the inscription of borders and purities and national identities and proper ethnicities on any place. It's something that I have a—you know, I'm an immigrant from Canada to France with a British passport, so I've had an extremely privileged experience of immigration, with only a little shaky territory, because of Brexit: what's going to happen to my ability to work in France or elsewhere in Europe? It's not clear. So I have these little wobbly areas, but perhaps this opens up a desire to understand more about the actual traumas of people who are moving from place to place, from South to North. Undoubtedly, I'm projecting a kind of utopian feeling onto Troubadour and Cathar culture, which in certain ways is a misrepresentation. But it's also a desire to want to understand the place I am in, in relation to the history of the mythologizing of that place, and also to understand the place I come from through the lens of where I'm now living. In a really strange way, as a Canadian settler, whose family arrived there roughly between the early eighteenth and the early twentieth centuries, I'm only slowly coming into a realization of what that history might mean, and what it might mean to be complicit with something that one absolutely disagrees with. I'm learning about my Canadian settler history from the point of view of being situated in the old Aquitaine region, and learning about the formation of France via the excision of heretical, secular, and transcultural movements in medieval thinking and culture.

[Liz,] I loved this phrase you used, "Women laying down their account," in terms of the weaving culture, which I brought up a couple of times. It's something I'm just learning about in this field of medieval song, the presence of women's weaving songs as being maybe one of the threads which fed into early troubadour practice. A lot of these early women's weaving songs were highly erotic—it was women singing together as they embroidered and wove. They're really ribald. They're excessive—and not in what we might now might call heteronormative ways. It's desire shooting all over the place, like messy threads, so there's that. And there's the fact that the Cathars were known to be itinerant weavers. One of the accounts of the Albigensian Crusade that I was reading suggested that one part of the French Crown's desire to exterminate the culture and economy of that region was to bring the weaving industry to the north of France. So they ended the weaving industry in Aquitaine, and then the Normandy area became the weaving center of what became France. So there's this whole thing about weaving as well, which is a creator of value. It's the appropriation of weaving by some proto-capitalists' desires to own the means of production.

OK, that's a whole grab bag of responses. I have a strong desire to continue to try to think the question of Indigeneity in an extremely diverse way, and by diverse I mean . . . I've been interested in Deleuze and Guattari's work on the refrain in *A Thousand Plateaus*, and they begin by talking about the refrain and birdsong and territory, and birdsong as consolidating a territoriality, and there being a competitive aspect among male birds. They're declaring the borders of their zones of eating and reproducing. It was a very gnarly text to read because I disagreed with virtually everything they said. But then, of course, you get—they're so classically French—you get to the end of their description of territory, and I'm going, "It doesn't always work that way. It's not territory." And then they talk about refrain as a line of flight outside of territory—which is what interests me! And this idea of a line of flight as having a long duration, where cultures and peoples, and mixtures of cultures and peoples in movement, can be taken into this thread ground, is something that seems extremely necessary to me personally. I don't yet know how to accomplish that other than reading and learning and talking together and asking questions and . . . I think I'll leave it at that.

Judith: So do people have responses to this?

Lisa: I'm just going to repeat this great phrase of Liz's. She was just talking about the nightingale's severed tongue murmuring on the earth: "Entropic remainder nevertheless nutritive."

Steve McCaffery: Lisa, you know there is a severed tongue on the front cover of the *Open Letter* "Canadian @Pataphysics" issue.

Lisa: No way!

Steve: And it's actually taken from emblem books. It's quite wonderful the way that body parts become emblematized in the seventeenth century. That's one thread. Yeah . . . I actually had a thought going back to your wonderful talk, Lisa; you brought up the notion of the paragram. Two things came up in my mind at that point. The first one was Baudrillard's wonderful chapter on the extension of the name of God in *Symbolic Exchange and Death*, in which he does a very different reading of the paragram and rhyme, in terms of the word and the anti-word, and it works to a mutual cancellation. Basically, what he's saying is Saussure was seeing Aphrodite placed within these texts, and that Saussure himself basically gave up the project because he started reading Aphrodite in the *Geneva Gazette*. Everywhere you look is—

Lisa: Paul Zumthor has this—there's a feeling that he thinks it's a little bit of a joke, what [Saussure's] doing . . .

Steve: Right, yeah. But I think the Baudrillard is very interesting in the way of rethinking it. I think the way you presented it as a way of altering, of decelerating or breaking the flow of meaning, was absolutely fantastic. But then thinking about Baudrillard's notion of cancel, erasure, and movement out—I think that the whole trope of a cancellation haunted me in many of the things that you were saying about the subsong. Why is the subsong sub? And also—

Lisa: Why is the subsong sub?

Steve: Yeah. And the thing you were saying about the loss of cultural memory and the rebirth of memory is hugely important. And the other point I thought of, Lisa, was the whole notion of wordplay within Occitan poetry. In your talk, you talked a lot about William of Aquitaine's use of *joi* and *amor*. And *amor* is love, in reverse is Roma, which is Vatican, which is everything that's complete opposition is there.

Lisa: Yeah, that's part of it.

Steve: I believe that level of play is there.

Lisa: It's absolutely, dare I say, central, to what they do. I can't remember her name right now, but I read a book by a woman scholar of Troubadour poetry writing in English that was about the idea of play in the poetry. [Laura Kendrick, *The Game of Love: Troubadour Word Play* (Berkeley: University of California Press, 1988).] The songbooks that we have date from the thirteenth century, through to the sixteenth, maybe? That's where the body of 2,600 poems is found, and they are in different libraries—there are some in the Bibliothèque Nationale in Paris. There's one in Modena in Italy [Il Canzoniere Provenzale Extense], in Biblioteca Estense, and some in other places. Scholars go to these archives to consult these songbooks, and they compare versions, and so forth. I've only seen a facsimile of one of those songbooks, and that was the Modena songbook, one of the very earliest ones, thirteenth-century, within the living memory of the Crusade. And in it, the breaks between words happen at completely standard places. We agree that a word is a unit, and so fallaciously, we think of the word as a sign, etc. And that word has a beginning and end, and then there's another word, and we conventionally put a space between words. Well, she says that in the precodified written drafts and versions of poems, there wasn't, at that point, a convention. Or there was a choice to stretch and challenge conventions of spaces between words, and so letters were the letters, say, of a phrase, and were clustered in different ways, so that the breaks didn't come between what we would consider to be words. And this meant that somebody who was reading or memorizing or learning from a script, or writing the script, would hear and see and experience different, simultaneous clusterings of meaning. An example she gave—which was really funny, so it stuck in my head—was this. Recently, there has been a contemporary opera based on Jaufre Rudel, who was famous for his song, "love from afar," "l'amour de loin." This word *loin* in French is L-O-I-N. I looked up the Occitan word for *loin*, and it's *lonh*. L-O-N-H. And she explained how depending where you put spaces in this word, and also according to the sounds on either side of it, this cluster of sounds that add up to the word *lonh* could mean not only distance, but could mean—very often meant—"ointment," and that this ointment was completely understood to be erotic juice, and medical salve, and also a spiritual kind of salve. So all these different kinds of juice were circulating in the idea of distance. Anybody hearing *lonh* would be simultaneously hearing and processing these other juices. So that was an example she gave of how clustering letters and sounds and phonemes—against the grain of how we now isolate word from word with spaces between—encouraged and tended to multiply meanings, many of which would seem to go against the grain of what might be considered the pheno-song or pheno-text.

Judith: Which is also very much connected to what you have been saying about rhyme, and the way that rhyme breaks up a text into phrases, patterns of stress that are quite interpretable, so that you see it really differently.

Lisa: Yeah, you hear things you don't know you're hearing really.

Julie Joosten: Yeah, I was just thinking about how each of you were speaking about images of the subtext, right? So you have this thinking that's happening in the image, the tongue that's returning to the earth, or the figure of the nightingale. What all of the images have in common is that they're images that refuse the monolingualism of senses, so suddenly you have a nightingale that is an image for a particular sound, and it makes me think also of *Samson Agonistes*, from Milton. When [Samson's] blinded, he says, "The sun to me is dark and silent as the moon," and there's this beautiful moment in Wordsworth, where the solitary reaper comes across the field, and he sees a woman singing, and he says, "I saw her singing." And there's something that I think is happening with rhyme there, too, where you hear it and you *see* it, and there's no way to separate out those senses. They occur as the carnal subsong, that is your body at the time and your modes of perception, which become modes of being, right? As this style of being.

Lisa: Yeah, and there's also a physiological proprioceptive relation. Your tongue is a meat muscle making the sounds, and so your tongue refines this position. There's a kind of muscle memory.

Julie: Yeah, and we think of muscles as willed, right? But, in fact, muscles are not always the function of will. I think of, you know, a charley horse, or a tremor, or an orgasm, right?

Lisa: Or even swallowing. It's really basic. Not that I'm against ecstasy or loss of control, but to swallow, to breathe—this is smooth muscle, involuntary muscle movement. So, yeah, I really hear what you're saying. Something I'm interested in thinking about lately is—I guess a perversion of the idea of an *image*, what it's become in mass media, in general culture. We imagine an image as being visual, but the imagination is not only a visual organ. In early thinking about the place of imagination in cognition and memory, the imagination was a place where different senses mixed and inflected one another. I have a lot of interest in returning that mess of sensing to the image.

It's great you bring up this phrase, "the refusal of monolingualism," because, even apart from sensing and the image, that's something we've been talking about, especially Shannon and me. Did you want to say something about refusal of monolingualism?

Shannon: We were talking before we came here—I was saying that one of the classes that I teach is Canadian literature, and that the first exercises I do with my students in this class—it's a foundations class, so second year—is a listening exercise. I ask them to try to keep their voices filling the room and to call out all of the names of the languages they have competencies in. In both cases that I've done this, the room is filled with many different voices—it goes on for quite a long time, and there are so many different languages that are available in the room, just with the students in there, and it's a class of usually sixty or seventy students. It gives us a very different idea of sonic texture or linguistic texture—it's really polylingual. But then I say to them, "So this large textbook that we have here, what language do you think most of the texts—well, *all* of texts—you'll encounter in this are going to be?" And, of course, in Canadian literature—we're not even talking about Québécois literature most the time, unless it's in translation. We're dealing with monolingualism at a state level.

One of the things your talk provoked, and that our conversations around it have provoked, is of breaking away from a linear historical notion that's colored by, as you say, mythology like Anglo-Saxonism. The idea of recovering Anglo-Saxon textuality in order to promote a monolingual state, nation state, or idea of an ideal past, Golden Age, where everything was more English, or so on—can be broken, in terms of actually registering the polylingualism that you talk about. I'm thinking now about the nightingale as an improvisatory bird that poets learn from, that there was almost a jazz back and forth . . . And you were telling me about a word?

Lisa: Yeah, there was an Occitan word that I came across in Rudel, *jauzen*, joyous, and I'm super-curious what, if any, the relationship of *jazz* to *jauzen* is? The other word you mentioned earlier was *improvisation*, and I think it's really interesting to think of polylingualism almost in relationship to improvisation, polylingualism as being improvisational. Because we think of language in terms of expertise—am I good enough to speak this language? Am I bilingual? Or trilingual? How many languages *do* you speak? This could be something really typical for a North American to ask a European: "Oh, wow! You speak four languages. I only speak one language or one and a half." So we kind of *count* languages, but the reality of vital, healthy language use is that people move between languages and mix them according to whom they're with, and what the situation is, and what is the mode of address for this space, the given space that's being inhabited. So it's really got nothing to do with what we might consider to be proficiency; it has to do with recognition of whom you're speaking with, and the desire to enter a linguistic field that's in movement.

Shannon: And then you have the echo of the letter . . .

Lisa: Yeah, people speak languages that they don't necessarily know very well, and that's something I've learned about polylinguality that I would like to learn more about and think in a more politicized way.

Judith: Especially transgenerationally, where you might have a huge amount of feeling association attached to a particular word or a language that you don't know very well, and that would, improvisatorially, enter into your speech somehow.

Cheryl Emerson: Two things have been running through my mind. First, when we talk of monolingualism, I have to think of Derrida's *Monolingualism of the Other; or, The Prosthesis of Origin* and the prosthetic aspect of all our language. The second thing I'm thinking is we've talked about an amateur reader, but aren't we amateur speakers in situations like these—we are not professional speakers. My grasp of French right now—I've just recently read *Paraguayan Sea*, and I think of [Erín] Moure's translation, and how amateur she is as a being, as a self, to begin with. There seems to be something mixing around with this polylingualism and amateur speakers. Maybe we could let ourselves off the hook—I'm embarrassed to utter a word, to pronounce a word out loud in French because it's not perfect. Bits of it can float around in my brain, but Lord forbid it actually come out of my mouth.

Lisa: A: I think that's something that most of us can relate to. B: I think it is definitely a form of linguistic colonization, to make people think that they're not good enough to speak, whatever the language, whatever the setting. This is one of the ways we're kept in place and, almost worse than that, it's one of the ways that we're prevented from connecting with other people.

Steve: I think the necessary inflection here is gesture. I think gesture is something that both supersedes speech and lingualism. I'm thinking about how you can be in a Japanese restaurant in Tokyo or an Icelandic restaurant in Reykjavík, and if you want to pay the bill, you make a gesture. And I think that universality of gesture is important to keep in mind. In terms of the development of languages, one idea is that primitive languages were gestural, and we moved from the gesture into sign systems.

Judith: We have time for maybe one or two more thoughts comments or questions . . . I wanted to ask one more thing, going
back to thinking about rhyme and temporality, to ask if you could
expand a little bit. Shannon, maybe this is also related to what
you were saying about the sestina, as well—but the idea of the
way that rhyme is multitemporal and nonlinear, in the sense that
if you hear a rhyme unexpectedly, you're sent back to the first
place that you heard that sound, and then you're also propelled
forward to think about when you're going to hear that sound
again. And you get trapped—well, you're not trapped, but you
get sent into a kind of echo chamber—where you're looking for
that sound, and the way that it creates meaning is an incredibly
productive way of playing with language that's built into language.

Shannon: I was thinking about the sestina. The sestina is a form
that operates on the echo. What makes the sestina is echo between
stanzas, in that space there. So there is a way that those six end
words (which in my case become titles for long poems) in a set
pattern creates the unfaithfulness of the word as well. Catachresis.
And an echo-engine.

Lisa: I like the idea of echo as unfaithful. That's another form of
heresy, in a sense.

Shannon: Yeah, and perversion.

Liz: I play a lot with form in my book, in individual poems and
with the book as a whole. I have a series of what I call recombi-
native sonnets, and what I wanted to do was—I love things like
dendrochronology, reading tree rings and core samples. Being able
to take a read of time in a physical thing has blown my mind since
childhood, and I wanted to do this in my poetry, in my book.
I thought of the form of a sonnet having fourteen lines, where
each line would be composed using a different sort of constraint,

but it'd be composed of content from the first fourteen poems in the book. So there would be a return, a reencountering of the material. In your mind, you're reexperiencing the past. I've had interesting reactions to the book. Sort of like, "What were you doing? You're doing something, you're messing with me."

Lisa: They hear the repetition without understanding they've heard the repetition . . .

Liz: Yeah, people who aren't overly familiar with experimental poetry, or this kind of poetics, they're kind of—they're *onto you*, but they don't understand the witchiness of it.

Judith: So that's a tree-ring sonnet, right? It's going through the book, in each layer of the column. It's really amazing . . .

I think we should end here, so that we can take a little break before the reading. Thank you.

Notes

1. This transcript has been lightly edited to eliminate minor redundancies and dysfluencies, to make it easier to follow in print form. In all other respects, the text transcribes the original utterances as they happened in conversation as faithfully as possible. Many thanks to Jake Reber for making the initial transcription.

Contributors

Judith Goldman is associate professor of English and director of the Poetics Program at University at Buffalo. She is author of four books of poetry: *Vocoder* (2001); *DeathStar/rico-chet* (2006); *l.b.; or, catenaries* (2011); and *agon* (2017). In 2018–2019, she collaborated on two full-gallery museum shows featuring large format, digital-print hybrid artist books of her poetry exploring five hundred years of British and US cultural history around the Northwest Passage and Open Polar Sea, together with contemporary Polar tourism, shipping, extractive capitalism, and climate science. She writes criticism on contemporary American poetry and serves as Poetry Features editor for *Postmodern Culture.*

Liz Howard is a poet, editor, and educator. Her first collection, *Infinite Citizen of the Shaking Tent,* won the 2016 Griffin Poetry Prize and was shortlisted for the 2015 Governor General's Award for Poetry. Her second collection, *Letters in a Bruised Cosmos,* was shortlisted for the 2022 Griffin Poetry Prize and the Trillium Poetry Prize. She joined Concordia University's Department of English as an assistant professor of creative writing in June 2023. Born and raised on Treaty 9 territory in Northern Ontario, she currently lives in Toronto.

Shannon Maguire's published volumes of poetry include *Myrmurs: An Exploded Sestina and fur(l) parachute.* Maguire edited and wrote the critical introduction to *Planetary Noise, Selected Poetry of Erín Moure*. Maguire has served as assistant professor (Limited Term Appointment) of Creative Writing at University of Calgary from 2016–2018 and has taught courses in creative writing, academic writing, gender in Shakespeare, and literary theory at Algoma University. Maguire holds an MFA in creative writing from the University of Guelph and an MA in English from Brock University.

James Maynard is curator of the Poetry Collection, the library of record for twentieth- and twenty-first-century poetry in English, and coordinator of the Rare and Special Books Collection at the University at Buffalo (UB) Libraries. He has published widely on and edited a number of collections relating to the poet Robert Duncan, including *Ground Work: Before the War/In the Dark* (2006), *(Re:)Working the Ground: Essays on the Late Writings of Robert Duncan* (2011), *Robert Duncan and the Pragmatist Sublime* (2018), and *No Hierarchy of the Lovely: Ten Uncollected Essays and Other Prose 1939–1981* (2020). His edition of *Robert Duncan: Collected Essays and Other Prose* (2014) received the Poetry Foundation's Pegasus Award for Poetry Criticism.

Steve McCaffery is a Canadian independent writer and multidisciplinary artist. Author of over forty-five books and chapbooks, his work has been translated into several languages including Chinese, Turkish, French, German, Portuguese, and Italian. His latest work is *Carnival: The Complete Version* published in 2022.

Jerome McGann is emeritus university professor, University of Virginia. In 2022 he published two books: *Culture and Language at Crossed Purposes: The Unsettled Records of American Settlement* and *Byron and the Poetics of Adversity*. He is currently editing Jaime de Angulo's *Old Time Stories* and preparing a critical study of the work's remarkable poetics.

Lisa Robertson is a Canadian poet, art writer, and novelist who lives in France. She has published nine books of poetry, most recently *Boat* (2022); three books of essays; and one novel, as well as contributing to many artists' catalogs and monographs. Her books *Starlings* (poems, 2017) and *Anemones: A Simone Weil Project*, an annotated translation of Weil's 1942 essay on the troubadour poets and the Cathar heresy (2021), are the most recent outcomes of *wide rime*, her ongoing study of troubadour poetics. In 2017 she was awarded an Honorary Doctorate in Letters by Emily Carr University of Art and Design, and in 2018 the Foundation for the Contemporary Arts in New York awarded her the inaugural C. D. Wright Award in Poetry.

Nikolaus Wasmoen is visiting assistant professor of English and Digital Scholarship at the University at Buffalo where he teaches literature, digital humanities, and media studies. Wasmoen earned his PhD in English from the University of Rochester, where he completed his dissertation, *Editorial Modernism: T. S. Eliot, Marianne Moore, Ezra Pound*. He is the technical director for the Marianne Moore Digital Archive, the technology and infrastructure chair for the Modernist Studies Association, and the Association for Documentary Editing's liaison to the Modern Language Association.

Index